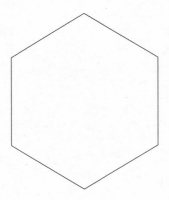

The Simplicity Principle

Six steps towards clarity
in a complex world

Julia Hobsbawm

KoganPage

Publisher's note
Every possible effort has been made to ensure that the information contained in this book is accurate at the time of going to press, and the publishers and author cannot accept responsibility for any errors or omissions, however caused. No responsibility for loss or damage occasioned to any person acting, or refraining from action, as a result of the material in this publication can be accepted by the publisher or the author.

First published in Great Britain and the United States in 2020
by Kogan Page Limited

2nd Floor, 45 Gee Street	122 W 27th St, 10th Floor	4737/23 Ansari Road
London	New York, NY 10001	Daryaganj
EC1V 3RS	USA	New Delhi 110002
United Kingdom		India

Kogan Page books are printed on paper from sustainable forests.

ISBN   978 1 7896 6355 6
E-ISBN 978 1 7896 6353 2

British Library Cataloguing-in-Publication Data
A CIP record for this book is available from the British Library.

Library of Congress Control Number
2019059213

Typeset by Integra Software Services, Pondicherry
Print production managed by Jellyfish
Printed and bound by CPI Group (UK), Croydon CR0 4YY

To Jessica Morris, Hexagon Thinker par excellence and
founder of OurBrainBank, for her simple courage.
And to the memory of Tommy Helsby, much missed.

The best bee in the world can teach
only what she herself knows.

JULIEN FRANÇON

CONTENTS

PREFACE

Life is really simple, but we insist on making it complicated.

CONFUCIUS

I wrote *The Simplicity Principle* to reconnect us to human-scale, human-level solutions in a superfast machine-filled world, and to pass on what I have learned and what I practise myself. Where possible I follow my own principles. When I do, I feel clearer, more creative, productive and on track. When I don't, I immediately know it – like a week without exercise or a holiday blowout on all the wrong foods.

Simplicity is an age-old concept. Back in the 14th century the British logician and Franciscan friar William of Occam stated that that simple works better than complicated. This clever chap wrote that *Numquam ponenda est pluralitas sine necessitate* which for those of you who, like me, did not advance hugely in Latin at school translates as 'Never undertake plurality without necessity'. This has become known as 'Occam's razor'. I think it is a pretty good 14th-century summary of this book.

Even further back in time the Greek philosopher Aristotle described *Eudaimonia*, which conveys a sense of happiness or blessedness – a thriving in the world. When you flourish, everything fits together, everything flows and just works, even if you are not completely sure why. Like a sixth sense, you just *know* when something is right, and it's a simple, certain feeling. In the modern world we talk less about flourishing and more about 'resilience'– as if we must survive rather than thrive. It is hard to flourish in a world beset by speed, scale, stress and uncertainty. Everywhere we look we can see the hallmarks of progress mixed with setback for humans. We are caught in a web of complexity, binding us tightly into systems and layers which can feel suffocating. It has become normal to manage a blizzard of codes and passwords, and to hold in balance being offline and online as if we are all experienced jugglers. Is it normal? Well, the new-normal. But it is often complicated.

Not that the quest for simplicity is only about mastering our use of technology. No one is saying that complexity began with the internet: certainly not me. We humans make what we use, and even the new generation of artificial intelligence and robotics will be largely designed, built and monitored by us. The change – if we want to make it – is not modern, high-tech and expensive. It is ancient, low-tech and every one of us can afford it: we can think about and do things differently.

This book is a 'how to', not just for individuals but for teams, for leaders and all those who, like me, chew on the endless toffee-stick of complexity where we know, deep down, that it *doesn't have to be like this*. Whatever you do in life, whether you are a student, a business leader, a manager, a freelancer, a parent juggling children and work, or newly retired, I wrote this book for you. I wrote this to help you break free of too much choice and complexity, and to help you gain control of your focus and productivity.

I wrote this book for myself, to keep me connected to the simplicity I crave in a happy but overloaded life. Like you, I have different roles and responsibilities. Like you, I realize that the idea of 'productivity' is not about working all the hours available, and not about being 'always-on', but finding the balance between work life and home life. I have used over 30 years of experience as a consultant, entrepreneur and educator, learning as I listen to others about what they want to cut through complexity. The result is this, the Simplicity Principle.

My proposition is simple. Complexity does not have to dominate, complicate or clutter our lives. We can learn to streamline and simplify what we focus on and where we place our energy and intelligence instead. I want to share with you my ideas for keeping things simple in all manner of situations and help you cut through complexity. The Simplicity Principle is based on two central ideas summed up in six words: **Keep it simple. Learn from nature.**

1   **Keep it simple.** Simplicity cuts through complexity. It brings focus, productivity, creativity and calm. Life is always going to be complicated, but we make it *way* more complicated than it needs to be. When we look around us, some of the basic systems of daily life, student life, working life and civic life are a tangle and jumble of 'systems' which are like a badly wound ball of wool. Simplicity brings balance between what is *complicated* – what can be laboriously unpicked – and what is *complex*, for which we need workarounds. It's time to push back. There are *always* things we can do to simplify and our ability to do so is often the difference between failure and success.

2   **Learn From Nature.** We can look and learn from nature and science in order to use pattern in a simple way in a process I call **Hexagon Action**. The six-sided hexagon shape we see in the snowflake, hexagonal atoms surrounding carbon (one of life's key building blocks) and the bee honeycomb show us the simplicity and usefulness of shape. Meanwhile, the number 6 itself is the so-called 'perfect number' in mathematics and is a useful organising number we can use. The six-sided hexagon is the poster-shape for simplicity. We can learn from its incredible strength and usefulness. And the poster-species for Hexagon Action is the honey bee. Like us it is a 'social' species and a 'superorganism' which depends on others to be its best self.

These six words – **Keep it simple, Learn from nature** – are the Simplicity Principle in a nutshell.

Flourish through simplicity

Putting the Simplicity Principle into practice should *feel* simple and it should feel *right*. It may not always be easy: thinking and changing behaviour requires commitment, curiosity, trial and error. But there is nothing complicated about it. There is nothing to pay, other than the price of this book. There is nothing to memorize, nothing to work at. Just see what triggers recognition or excitement and see what you want to try out for as little as six minutes, six hours or six months.

Using the techniques outlined in these pages, I hope that you can flourish again. Perhaps you will even experience a sense of flourishing for the first time. Of course, if you think that your life is fine as it is, perhaps busy but not overloaded, or richly rewarding rather than frustrating, or if you already have a system to get through 'stuff' in your life, then save yourself some valuable time and put this book down! But of course I hope you *do* read on, so I can share not just my ideas but some interesting findings about how we think and behave which you might find useful. I hope that you will find the Simplicity Principle useful as I'm all for doing as well as thinking, for action. So I hope that the system of Hexagon Action will become as useful to keeping your life and career on track as keeping to 10,000 steps a day, or consuming five-a-day of your fruit and vegetables. The Simplicity Principle is about a new kind of health, wellbeing and fitness which takes place outside of the gym. It is part of what I call Social Health, which is how we connect to our lives, each other and technology in the digital era.

By reading on, you're going to find out what it can be like to radically simplify the way you look at your life, give your head space and raise your productivity and focus – in a very straightforward way. Shall we begin?

Introduction

Simple can be harder than complex: you have to work hard to get your thinking clean to make it simple. But it's worth it in the end because once you get there, you can move mountains.

STEVE JOBS

It started with a KISS

I first came across the idea of simplicity in a complex world in my twenties, back in the 1980s, when life seemed a lot more straightforward and uncomplicated than it is today. I was just starting out in my career, and I worked in book publishing in a tiny publisher called Virago where I had the privilege of working with the great American poet, academic and civil rights campaigner Maya Angelou. She made a lasting impression on me.

Maya stood well over six feet tall and had the most stunning baritone voice and incredible stage presence. When she spoke, you listened. In private, she was a big fan of reciting aphorisms. She did this with a flourish, usually with a smile, often with a whisky, always with seriousness. As a poet she understood that simplicity often has the best impact. I always remember her correcting someone for saying 'I'll be brutally honest.' 'Why,' she asked, 'do you need to add in being brutal? Isn't honesty enough on its own? Just say you'll be honest without complicating it. Keep it simple, sweetie.'

That referred to one of Maya's favourite sayings. You may know KISS as standing for *Keep It Simple, Stupid*. But because she disliked vulgarity or indeed brutality of any kind, Maya Angelou used her poetic licence to amend it slightly. Her amended version of KISS was even better: the 'sweetie' was a big improvement on 'stupid'. *Keep It Simple, Sweetie*: I like that.

Either way, KISS is as serious as it is simple. Although I look back now and think life, pre-internet, pre-social media was simpler, of course it wasn't. It was just different. Charles Dickens wrote in the 19th century of Britain 'being bound hand and foot in red tape'. Actual red tape still exists in the legal profession all over the world: documents are still bound up in a hangover from those times when complexity arose from our attempts to impose social and political order with taxes, laws and financial 'instruments'. Today complexity envelops us like a tight scarf, even in everyday tasks. It is invisible and yet drains time, energy and focus. We can see and feel the effects of too little KISS and too much complexity all too clearly.

The US Army knew this all too well. KISS was first coined as a design principle in the 1930s by an American aerospace engineer at the famous Lockheed Skunk Works. Clarence 'Kelly' Johnson oversaw production of planes in World War II which were make-or-break not just for their pilots, but their country. He knew what a life-saving shortcut the principle of keeping things simple and focused was. He knew too that you had to design and build for simplicity, or his pilots could well be blown out of the sky.

Killer complexity

What a pity the KISS principle is no longer in popular usage today. In fact, we so take complexity for granted, simplicity has all but been forgotten. It certainly is no longer a priority. I wonder whether KISS was in action when two Boeing 737 MAX planes crashed in 2018 and 2019. A total of 346 people lost their lives and it immediately became clear that there had been a terrible complexity around both humans and technology which might have played a part. In the aftermath it turned out that both humans and machines were to blame. There was a design flaw in the new cockpit computer system, and when this combined with inexperienced pilots given very little training in the new system it proved catastrophic. The computer flaw started to push the plane nose-down and override pilot efforts to bring it back up. I would argue that when the KISS principle is overlooked it can genuinely be disastrous.

The CAT versus the KISS

I often think of the pilots, in their frantic confusion, and I recall a syndrome I notice in clients of mine in less desperate circumstances who are nevertheless hampered by a tangle of trouble. They often feel bound up by competing issues, their focus stressed. I call this the CAT syndrome which stands for Complexity, Anxiety and (too little) Time. No one can think straight if they are in the middle of something they just don't understand. Pressure to perform makes things worse, and if there is a deadline it makes disaster inevitable. The lesson? Don't sideline simplicity.

What about everyday life? Where's the simplicity there? Life doesn't feel simple when you are opening different windows-within-windows, or trying to find the perfect battery charger, or making sure that your document is compatible, or wondering why that 10 minutes you thought you were spending online has become an hour. If you feel you have to make yourself visible every few minutes on social media, or to master the latest technology in your office just to keep up, this is at the very least a time-suck. But out there in everyday life on the street, it can be even more complicated. I was in New York once when the lights went out around Times Square for several hours due to a power outage. Something to do with a substation. Several thousand people were affected, with hundreds stuck on dark subways or in elevators, while cars had to dodge out of action traffic lights. Everyone relied on battery life in mobile phones to power any communication but no one really knew what was happening. Yet this was in Manhattan, home to the United Nations! Home to Wall Street, to Broadway. Frank Sinatra sang 'If I can make it there, I can make it anywhere' about this city! And it happened in the middle of the 21st century! A month later, I was one of a million people in the UK who lost all electricity for several hours when the National Grid experienced a power surge. Failure of modern life to behave as it should is always quite a wake-up call and always creates anxiety and disquiet beyond the event itself. It reminds us how reliant we are, how we have no real backup plan. Not in our heads and not really in the world. We feel powerless and it is not a good feeling.

In the aftermath of these system failures of course no one individual is to blame. Only a bunch of complex computer systems. They are hyperconnected but not human. They have no face and no voice. The chain of command to them is so wide and deep it is never easy to pinpoint who is in control, let alone who is to blame. When one link goes down, we are instantly plunged back in a time warp to the centuries before everything we take for granted today: electricity, mass transport, aircon, traffic lights or TV.

There is not much simplicity in our public life either. Today's politicians can't seem to explain their own policies and systems to people without getting tied up in knots. Ahead of the Brexit referendum in the UK in my home country in 2016 the *Financial Times* said that everything to do with relations between Great Britain and the European Union involved 'tortuous complexity'. In the vote itself people confounded political expectations and voted to leave. The winning campaign condensed all that complexity into a simple, winning message: 'Take back control'. The campaign was led by Boris Johnson who went on to become Prime Minister and then to win a huge majority at the 2019 General Election with the slogan 'Get Brexit done'. People want to cut through complexity like Occam's razor and reward politicians who recognize this. Critics call this simplistic populism but it may in fact be realism.

This book is all about turning on its head the assumption that all things complicated have to be like that, always. And to make sure we remember that the human in the Machine Age is still in the driving seat. The systems we create and follow are ours, and how we behave can change in small, purposeful, daily ways.

The most complicated system in the universe

Of course, life is complicated. You don't strike me as the kind of reader who needs things sugar-coated or made simplistic. Humans are about as sophisticated and complex as it gets. We have 86 billion neurons firing all the time in our brain, which has been rightly described as 'the most complicated object in the known universe'.[1] The brain is part of an even more staggeringly complicated body which has nearly 40 trillion cells inside it, keeping the show of being alive on the road, every second of every day. We have evolved over millions of years to overcome the challenges of nature and disease (from ice ages to plagues), wars and scarcity to build societies, cities, computers, robots and nanotechnology.

But our ability to create complexity is at complete odds with the simple needs we have emotionally and physically: once we have love, shelter, food and work, we don't need much else, and yet in order to get any or all of these, life is increasingly complicated. And here's the irony: one of the reasons we struggle with complexity is that our brains are not wired to handle excess information and our ability to cope with excessive stimulation is in fact very limited. Our brains may be incredible feats of natural engineering but our working memory – that part of our mental processing which governs reasoning and behaviour – typically shows a limit of between four and seven items at any one time.[2] That would be fine if we were all still hunting and gathering like we did 200,000 years ago, in tiny cut-off communities, doing seven things or less over a lifetime: making families, fighting, cooking, hunting, staying alive. It's less good in a world where we make 35,000 decisions in a single day, where by 2021 the internet will create 3.3 zettabytes. There is no way I can put simply the unit of information (a zettabyte is equal to one sextillion or 1,000,000,000,000,000,000,000 bytes) but I think you will agree that it is... a lot.

Complexity cut-off

All of this matters because neuroscience shows us that once things get too complicated, our brains effectively short-circuit and cut out. The rise in stress symptoms as well as the rise in demand for digital detox are all symptoms of a world which overvalues complexity and yet craves simplicity. When we are overloaded, we make mistakes. We get stressed. Depressed. Angry. Disappointed. We struggle. We are multitasking even though we are only wired mainly to monotask instead. Yes: as you zigzag in and out of different applications, with noise, visuals, endless flipping, you are defying your brain's basic chemistry which is screaming *Code Red!* when you do that. But we don't feel it's wrong, or that we have a choice.

We certainly have some choice. And that choice begins with whether or not we choose to keep things complicated, or whether we decide – as I hope you will – to look for the simpler way. Let me explain what to expect in this book and how you can help yourself, and others, to get a handle on complexity and put it to one side in favour of its better self: simplicity.

In Part One I will make the case for turning towards simplicity and away from complexity, and explain the **Simplicity Principle** itself and **Hexagon Action**. The two go together, like theory and practice. Chapter 1, Keeping your balance: The simplicity spectrum, starts by playing devil's advocate and asking what's wrong with complexity, given how complicated humans are, and shows how it's not one thing or another but finding a balance between them. Chapter 2 introduces Hexagon Action. Think of it as your toolkit (many nuts and bolts are hexagon-shaped) because hexagons are super-resilient, efficient and flexible. Chapter 3 delivers on the promise on the front of this book and introduces the six ways to find your focus and improve productivity, before we get to them in detail.

In Part Two I'll lay out the detail of the **Six Sides of Simplicity**. This is Hexagon Action in practice: each side begins with a six-word axiom or saying to focus on. You can just jump straight to these if you like, and see which ones give you a prickle of recognition and pique your interest. The first three, *Clarity*, *Individuality* and *Reset,* cover how to connect with priority and purpose, develop habit, overcome distractions, connect with creativity and wellbeing, and learn the value of disconnection when it comes to operating at your best. The second trio are *Knowledge*, *Networks* and *Time*. These ideas build on what I touched on in my last book, *Fully Connected: Social Health in an age of overload*. Social Health is a way to survive and thrive in the Internet Age.[3] At the beginning of each of the Six Sides of Simplicity are six short six-word simplicity mantras which summarize what's coming up. At the end of each section is a **Six-Fix** list of takeaways and calls to action for you which all focus on the six words at the heart of the Simplicity Principle: *keep it simple*, and *learn from nature*.

In Part Three you will meet some famous **Hexagon Thinkers** to inspire you, people who embody the spirit of the Simplicity Principle and practise Hexagon Action. And you will also get to Be the Bee: to imagine yourself in the roles which will help you plan to be your best connected, best productive and best individual self, just like the honey bee. I should say for any purist readers that sometimes I just say 'bee' but the specific species I mean is always the humble honey bee. Part Three also wraps up the book with some **Hexagon Action** exercises.

What does success look like?

Well, I hope you enjoy the stories and illustrations that show how using nature, geometry and pattern in the everyday and a little bit of honey bee tactics can retrain how you behave. What I call Social Health – connected behaviour in the Digital Age – depends on how well we manage what we do on- and offline, in and out of nature, and in either an organized or a disorganized way. Neuroscience – the study of our brains – is clear about how we can rewire both our thinking and our behaviour. We *can* unmake our patterns, change our paths: through neuroplasticity, that is the way brain constantly changes, we can relearn patterns of behaviour, of thinking, overlaying them with new techniques.[4] When you strip it down, when you give your task a KISS you're not going to go down the rabbit hole of limitlessness, which taxes your poor old brain. Instead, you're able to stand back, simplify and decide what's really the decisions and actions you need to make. In other words, you really can move mountains. It really is as simple as that.

PART ONE
Keep It Simple, Sweetie

1

Keeping your balance

The simplicity spectrum

For the simplicity that lies this side of complexity, I would not give a fig, but for the simplicity that lies on the other side of complexity, I would give my life.

OLIVER WENDELL HOLMES JNR

The needle in the haystack

Have you ever lost something and been completely unable to find it, even though you know it is *in there somewhere*? A friend of mine once had to unscrew her fireplace to access a passport which had fallen down the back, but this was more a case of literally misplacing something: knowing where it is and having to retrieve it. What about the times you just cannot access where something is because you have no system to find it? The idea of filing, a concept from the Middle Ages which means 'to string documents on a thread or wire to keep them in order', is quite simple: it is to *manage complexity*. There are more connected devices than people on the planet, and the volume of data being uploaded around the world each day is so fast and vast it is difficult to keep track (just by way of example 90 per cent of data on the internet has been added in the last five years).[1] The more we turn to technology and machines to help us manage the infinite, the less we rely on humans to keep what we learn, share, and use to manageable proportions.

This is a pity – and a mistake. It is true that humans have an in-built complexity bias, a natural inclination to make things complicated. As the design and engineering academic Don Norman writes in his book *Living with Complexity*:

> We seek rich, satisfying lives, and richness goes along with complexity. Our favourite songs, stories, games, and books are rich, satisfying, and complex. We need complexity even while we crave simplicity… Some complexity is desirable. When things are too simple, they are also viewed as dull and uneventful.[2]

And as the economist Tim Harford points out in his wonderful book *Messy*: 'From the vantage point of a nice corner office, some-one else's messy desk is an eyesore. For the senior manager, the lesson is simple: resist the urge to tidy up. Leave the mess – and your workers alone.'[3] Yet we also crave simplicity, from Occam's razor to KISS, but also via our deep attachment to ritual: from the particular habits we have with our cups of tea and coffee, to the global appeal of team sports with their rules, or indeed religious ritual and observance – and for many people, order and simplicity is highly calming and reaffirming.

The Simplicity Principle is all about getting the right balance between two extreme states and finding stability somewhere in the middle.

The balancing beam

Try and imagine yourself in the place of a gymnast poised on a single 4-inch-wide balance beam in gymnastics and having to jump, leap, turn and stand for 70–90 seconds, without wobbling or falling off. Nothing more to add: simple. Have you ever tried it? In fact, can you even contemplate it? Balance is essential in gymnastics and maintaining your centre of gravity is the principal rule. For seniors, stability can make the difference between a life of safety and one of falls. When my mother, aged 87, took a terrible tumble in her apartment and broke her thigh bone, it took six months of intensive physiotherapy focused on balance to get her walking again without assistance.

My mother had to do endless exercises in order to build up her strength, agility and her balance. These exercises were not random. They were based on deep knowledge and imposed structure and pattern. She kept photos of them on her wall to remind her and despite the severity of her injury, she did regain her balance. It took time, patience and a focus on simple, repeatable steps.

Selling simplicity

I know things can be downright difficult, but I never think they are impossible. Call me an optimist with a handle on pessimism! I know that simplicity works, and I look around and know that simplicity itself sells. Steve Jobs, founder of Apple, was right when he said that it's hard work to keep things simple. But he also made a fortune out of simplicity. He knew the rewards of it. Apple products put simplicity at the heart of their sleek, cool, functional design. They are simple to use, they are simple to look at, and they backup and store pretty simply. When you look at the list of the world's richest companies, from Amazon to Alibaba, from Johnson & Johnson to Tencent, they all share something in common: behind the scenes there is tremendous complexity to what they do, from the back-end technology, corporate structures and product ranges. But at the front end, what the consumer sees and experiences in order to browse, buy, choose and stay loyal has to be as simple as possible if it is to work. So, complexity is there, but it is not front and centre: that's the job of simplicity.

Simplicity sells everything from products to pop songs to politics. The message 'Take back control' won the Brexit referendum in Britain and 'Make America great again' was a winning slogan for President Trump in the United States. In both places lots of people sneered in exasperation and hated the simplicity, but it worked. It's called 'cut-through'. In India, dairy brand Amul's slogan is simply 'The Taste of India', while China Mobile's tagline is 'Reaching Out from the Heart'. Ed Sheeran's song *Shape of You* is Spotify's most-streamed song of all time and the hook 'I'm in love with the shape of you' is very simple. That's what a winning piece of music is: simple, memorable.

Life's hard and soft edges

Nature knows all about the spectrum between simplicity and complexity. In many ways it is hugely complex – just like our bodies and brains. The chaos theory which tells us that a butterfly flapping its wings has a micro-impact on a hurricane is part of the random, chaotic side of nature. However, while plenty of shapes and patterns in nature are what's called 'fractal' (like trees), nature also provides a counterbalance to the universe's chaos and complexity. It is full of shapes which follow rules and which have an order which can be mapped, understood and applied. The hexagon and all geometric shapes in nature impose design through their lines, and offer up something of a filing system, which can be efficient, organized and copied. By us.

Here is just one example: the honeycomb. This is the beating heart of a hive and contains bee larvae, pollen and honey. The cells are hexagonal and made of wax. The honeycomb is one of the most famous shapes in the whole of nature. The shape of the hexagonal cells never alters, as experiments to try and fool bees into making a different shape have shown. It was Charles Darwin who first claimed that the shape was to do with space efficiency, and while this is largely true, it turns out to be something else as well. In *The Life of the Bee*, a charming and exhaustive study published in 1901, Maurice Maeterlinck concludes that 'the hexagon is not merely the result of mechanical necessities, but that it has its true place in the plans, the experience, the intellect and will of the bees'.[4] I'll come back to the hexagon in more detail because it is the way in which we put the whole of the Simplicity Principle into practice: side by side, bit by bit.

The burdens of complexity

Using what we can learn from nature's use of pattern and shape helps us navigate through the complex and chaotic limit*less* over-load of the present. Instead of feeling at the mercy of chaos and *too much*, we can create workarounds to make the principle of simplic-ity easier than the burdens of complexity. The biggest and most obvious burden is on productivity and on our mental health. As technology speeds up our lives it also complicates them. You would think our lives, especially our working lives would be easier, but this is not the case at all. Globally, productivity levels, used to meas-ure how much workers contribute economically, are stagnant. In the UK where I live, The Health and Safety Executive reports (2019) that over 15 million working days each year are lost to stress,[5] while data from the European Commission (2000) shows that up to 60 per cent of all working days lost are due to stress.[6] Across the world, stress is a massive expense to business, costing $300 billion annually to the United States alone.[7] The World Health Organization reports one death from suicide every 40 seconds around the world.[8] It is now recognized that suicide is a social, societal problem, not just a private one limited to the individuals concerned.

It is no exaggeration therefore to say that stress is like an oil spill spreading out across society. Modern life has become too tough and too complicated for our own good. One of the reasons is that we are constantly told technology is making our lives easier, smoother and faster. Experience is often the opposite. Yes, society may be advancing in many welcome ways, but at a personal level, stress indicates that our lives feel anything but easy, or smooth.

Plain and simple

Of all the different definitions of simplicity, the one I like the most is this: 'the quality or condition of being plain or uncomplicated in form or design'. The author Matt Haig, who writes about mental health and anxiety, puts it well: 'After craving, for years, complexity and believing that that was futuristic... now, everyone's simply heading the other way.'[9] The stress of not being able to just get something done quickly, cleanly, meaningfully and instead be delayed, disappointed, disconnected from a solution are all things which put pressure and pain into people's personal psyche. No one wants to feel powerless. The challenge is to recognize complexity when we see it and find a way to personally side-step and cope when it is not working in our favour.

Complex versus complicated

Don't get me wrong. Complexity is inevitable and to some extent absolutely necessary. Medicine, quantum physics, robotics: these are not simple. Complex systems do work, a lot of the time, and they do bring us benefits. The scale of the challenge to simplify a complex world was put very well in a philosophy paper, back in 1962 in the *Journal of Philosophy*. The author, Mario Bunge, noted that:

If the theory of simplicity is to be of any use, it must cease avoiding complexities. The rule, 'Simplify', should not lead us to circumvent complexities by building ideally simple linguistic toys; theories of simplicity need not be simple themselves.[10]

What this means is that we must avoid being simplistic when trying to turn the complex into the simple.

It is worth saying again that 'complex' is not the same as 'complicated'. When something is complicated it means it is difficult to understand, but it can be unpicked and unpacked. A machine is a good example of something complicated. You can deconstruct something complicated, which makes managing it easier. Something complex – like a weather system or a human – is far more of a complex matter. There are lots of variables. One step even further than complexity is chaos, when you cannot predict or see around corners with any accuracy at all. Many people say this is, basically, life: get used to it. Well, yes, but don't drown in the sea of impossibility will you? Your brain, that wonderfully complex system, can learn, unlearn, and remake patterns of thinking constantly: you can adjust your thinking and behaving to prioritize one system over another.

Mirror, signal, manoeuvre

Take driving. Once you have learned to drive you tend not to forget it. But you had no idea initially. Your brain had to adapt to understanding a set of complicated tasks which have to be done at the same time. Being in charge of a moving machine and navigating other humans in other machines at speed is no small ask. Around the world over a million people a year die in road accidents, and a further 50 million people get injured.[11] This is because we don't do so well handling the complexity all the time. The cut-through for safety is a set of rules based on simplicity. In the UK, the mantra 'mirror, signal, manoeuvre' is drilled into every learner driver. In fact, that simple message asks people to accept and cope with the complexity of the road and keep their attention sharp. But mobile phones have complicated matters. The World Health Organization began warning long ago in 2011 of the dangers of 'driver distraction' caused by mobile phones.[12] Even more recent reports suggest that 25 per cent of accidents worldwide are caused by them. Why? I'm afraid that the answer is simple. Driving requires attention which cannot be diluted by multitasking. But in exactly the same way that we have deluded ourselves it's perfectly safe to text and drive, or even to fiddle with satnav, we do the same in everyday life: we try and do too much instead of making simple, straightforward focus a priority.

So, you get the picture. What I'm after is to reduce, manage and minimize complexity. This is the basis of the Simplicity Principle. And the first thing to do is to call it out.

The complexity test

I like the duck test, the proverb that says, 'If it looks like a duck, swims like a ducks, and quacks like a duck, it probably *is* a duck.' When it comes to complexity versus simplicity, it is usually obvious. Apply it to how complicated your life is right now. Is it tangled and mangled by too much to do? Is the world around you organized in a straightforward way or do you have layer upon layer of different people to 'go through' in order to get anything done? Do you have deadlines and timelines in different time zones? Do you have more than one 'device' and several different platforms you have to be on just to get through your day? That's sounding quite duck-like to me. Quack quack… you just passed the complexity test.

Let's take the duck test further. Answer these three questions and see how dominant complexity is in stressful or problematic situations. Tick which answer applies most to your view.

Take the test

1   How you think about your daily life

A   ○   It runs smoothly and cleanly: technology, people, systems. I feel lucky and grateful that modern life has got to this point.

B   ○   On a good day I feel productive and in control. But there is usually at least one thing which doesn't work so well: an app freezes or some kind of miscommunication happens on email or in a group chat which takes time to sort out.

C   ○   Pretty much every day I feel like I have to deal with 'life traffic jam' involving delays or difficulty. It could be people-led or machine-led. I don't feel in control of my life as much as I could or should be.

D   ○   I feel like a cog in a wheel. I feel forced to use technology to do everything from ordering shopping to reaching people and it gets me down. I feel dependent on others and not in any way an agent of my own life.

2   How you think about the way the world works

A   ○   Overall, it works well. Things run on time, and as long as the technology doesn't go down, life is fine. Yes, it's complicated, but that is the price we pay for everything being good around us.

B   ○   I am beginning to have my doubts. I know how far we've come but I see big problems around us which don't seem to be getting easier. I think the world is on the edge of chaos more than it should be.

C   ○   The problems around me are all to do with other people making mistakes or getting things wrong. No technological device takes away from human error and bad management. I feel resigned to having good days and bad days, just like I always did.

D ◯ Things are getting more complicated, not less. Nothing works in a simple way and the problems of the world don't seem to get solved at all. I feel very anxious and pessimistic about the way the world operates and people like me feel powerless.

3 You have an idea and want to put it into action at work

A ◯ That's straightforward. You can decide quickly and easily and have no levels or layers to go through (within reason) to make it happen. You have less than three people to consult or discuss with first.

B ◯ It is time-consuming and nothing can be done quickly or easily. However, you know a couple of people whom you could visit to charm and persuade to smooth the path for you.

C ◯ There is strict protocol and a system which involves putting something on paper and presenting it via committees which involve people you don't know. There are layers of 'leadership icing' which you are stuck under, as a 'marzipan manager'.

D ◯ Your workplace is not receptive to ideas and you have not got authority to generate solutions: you can only implement someone else's instructions. Individuality and creativity don't count – nor does calling it out.

How you answered

Mostly A: You are not only an optimist but life is full of things that can be simply solved. So now you need to work on identifying the essence of the simple hacks which help you and maybe you can help others.

Mostly B: You're kind of in between the optimist and the pessimist. You know things can be complicated but you also feel they do work quite a lot of the time. Your challenge is to identify weak links and work on getting them fixed around you.

Mostly C: Either you have a gloomy disposition or things around you do not work so well. It feels as if bureaucracy is a big part of your life and you can never act easily or comfortably without going through others.

Mostly D: You see the world as full of complexity and that may be because in your world it is. This is definitely something which you are not – sadly – alone in experiencing but it does mean that a change in perspective, and circumstances is needed. You can be the change – nothing is all hopeless!

Let's look in more detail at the shape of simplicity, the number six, and Hexagon Action itself. It's time to get out the toolkit and get working on making your life more straightforward.

2

Six packs

Introducing Hexagon Action

Hexagons occur naturally and were one of the first alternative geometries to be appropriated by architecture. Nature is full of sixes.[1]

GRAHAM McKAY

The perfect number

The hero for this book was Euclid of Alexandria. He was a mathematician born around 2,400 years ago in Ancient Greece. Many things we regard as modern and which are embedded in our culture and systems were created or developed here, in 'the cradle of civilization': amongst them democracy, philosophy, playwriting, and maths.

Euclid is key to the principle of simplicity because he is known as 'the father of geometry'. It is Euclid who discovered that six is the 'perfect' number[2] and it is Euclid who wrote a book called *The Elements*, which sets out five axioms or generally held truths and assumptions about shape.[3] These are:

1 A line can be drawn from a point to any other point.

2 A finite line can be extended indefinitely.

3 A circle can be drawn, given a centre and a radius.

4 All right angles are 90 degrees.

5 If a line intersects two other lines such that the sum of the interior angles on one side of the intersecting line is less than the sum of two right angles, then the lines meet on that side and not on the other side. (This is also known as the Parallel Postulate.)

I'm going to cheekily add a sixth axiom to Euclid's list, in honour of his perfect six: geometry brings simplicity. Because when you use lines and create boundaries and shape, working with numbers of edges and angles, you impose order and understanding. Euclid's elements, and his sense of six, make perfect, simple sense to me.

Actions speak louder than words

Hexagon Action is a concept rather than a rigid rule which uses the shape and sides of geometry to help us stay focused. Why? Because you can count and see the sides of a problem so much more clearly, and because a geometric shape like the hexagon stands for connection: a single hexagon isn't anything like as powerful as a whole stack of them. The idea of Hexagon Thinking has been used in design and education in particular, and very much focuses on the shape as a visual aid. I want however to focus on a practical use in everyday life, where you want the principle to put into practice. I love the phrase 'Actions speak louder than words' which dates back to the 17th century. In my favourite movie, *My Fair Lady*, Audrey Hepburn sings of her frustration that the men in her life don't abide by this rule. 'Words, words, words, I'm so sick of words!' she sings. 'Show me! Show me now!' Hexagon Action is shape, yes, geometry, yes, natural inspiration, yes – but it is also a call to action.

The power of six

It is no accident that I choose the hexagon to represent simplicity partly because it has six sides. You have probably read other books which say 'The Answer' lies in a certain number. Six is, as it happens, a bit special, and here's why. Quite apart from it being within what we know about the limits of working memory (remember, what we can hold in our heads is not really more than seven things at any given time), it is the first and smallest in the series of numbers which Euclid identified as 'perfect'.[4] The next one along is 28, which has its uses as an organizing number because that's roughly one month, but the one after that leaps to 496 (which I hope you agree is a rather large number to base an organizing system around).

Winnie-the-Pooh's creator A A Milne wrote a poem called 'Now We Are Six' which puts into words that lovely feeling you get as a child when you reach the age of six, and become just a tiny bit independent.[5] He calls it feeling 'as clever as clever'. Well, the number six is a clever number. We all live by multiples of it in our 24-hour days, our 12-month years, and our six-day working week. Six has a useful symmetry to it because it can divide in half and in thirds. Like the hexagon shape itself, it is incredibly versatile, flexible and strong.

Six is a mysteriously alluring number which it turns out a great many of us are transfixed by without really knowing why. The great British physicist and Astronomer Royal Martin Rees, writing in his book *Just Six Numbers: The deep forces that shape the universe*, identifies six numbers which range from measuring electrical forces holding atoms together to the number of spatial dimensions in our world which he says 'seem especially significant... accidents of cosmic history'.[6] For those who like their cult TV shows, the futuristic series *The Prisoner* focused on the man called Number 6 who used to protest his individuality with the cry 'I am not a number! I am a free man!' Without going all mystical on you, the fact is that six is present as a number right across vast tracts of nature, science, and culture, and you do not have to look very far to see it. Here are just six examples:

1   All insects have six legs, and there are six ranked 'kingdoms' in biology.

2   The brain, which is the essence of what makes us human, has six areas through which it specifically experiences and learns: *the lobes*; *motor cortex* and *somatosensory cortex*; *brain stem*; *the limbic system*; *cerebrum*; and *cerebellum*.

3   Six is also a highly relevant and symbolic number in religion and global culture. Islam has six Axioms of Faith while the Jewish Seder plate is divided into six separate parts to hold the six ceremonial foods: matzah, the *zeroa* (shankbone), egg, bitter herbs, *charoset* (paste) and *karpas* (vegetable). Although Christianity celebrates the seven days of creation, it is of course the sixth day on which humans were created. And in China, six is considered lucky because it symbolizes flow and being well-off.

4   Sport loves six. Tennis has six games a set. Volleyball has six players per team and the basketball ball in the women's game is designated 'size 6'. Even cricket, a game I confess I do not remotely understand despite very conscious effort, has six balls in an over. In India, where cricket is revered, the number 6 is special because it is regarded as lucky: 15 August is Independence Day there and numerologists cite $1 + 5 = 6$ as a reason why 6 and its derivative numbers like 3 are lucky for them.

5   The number of dots in a braille cell is, yes, six, and on a flight deck the fundamental instrument configuration is often referred to, like beer, as a 'six-pack'. In anthropology, traditionally we bury our dead six feet under.

6   Let us not forget, finally, that 'sixth sense' is associated with extrasensory perception, and trusting our instinct is a key aspect of the Simplicity Principle overall. Common sense and sixth sense: not a bad combination!

Hunting the hexagon

Let me tell you what drew me to the hexagon in the first place. The idea of creating a personal and business management system based around the number six and illustrating that number within a shape first came to me when I was writing my last book, *Fully Connected*, especially as I toured the world talking about it after publication.

My central idea in this book was something called Social Health which revolves around applying similar principles to looking after the state of connection – humans using technology – as we do to our physical and mental health. That while we monitor what we eat and how we work out and how much sleep we get, we some-how end up taking the foot off the brake when it comes to hours spent 'gorging' online, getting 'infobese' on endless overwhelming information.

There is a central simplicity to this idea which resonated with audiences, but I still needed to illustrate it super-clearly and explain how it could be put into practice. Pattern and shape have always interested me because I like design and architecture and because it is clear – back to Apple for instance – just how strongly we relate to simple structure and imagery. Also, I like the building blocks of an operation, being able to unpick and unpack rather precisely how things happen, and it is probably why I like running micro-businesses: you have to get involved at every level of the system yourself as an owner–manager. So I hunted around for what felt like the right shape and number, not least because when you give speeches and presentations you learn to hone everything down as tightly as possible and the old adage 'less is more' rings true.

I immediately thought of circles, because this is the shape which we most associate with the idea of networks and connection, both of which lie at the heart of my work. The five Olympic rings are one of the most memorable graphic designs in history, instantly recog-nizable, an interlocking system which is all about harmony, strength, cooperation, endurance. All good stuff. Except it felt wrong. Circles are a bit limitless: there is no end to circularity, and I have always felt that we need something to *contain* what we do and how we do it, not endlessly expand it. Also, the network science which I communicate about is less about infinite circles and more about edges and borders and where things intersect. Everything is connected, spreads, or is not contained by circles but by the edges of geometry. So I kept looking for my ideal shape. Through my interest in productivity and management, I kept asking what it is that makes people at work be effective and engaged – or not. What helps their 'flow' and what hinders it? I started to read up on the natural world and what happens there, and was stunned to find that insects, in particular termites, ants and bees, all display incredibly sophisticated means of organizing, building, cooperating and generally making things happen. I highly recommend Lisa Margonelli's book *Underbug* about studying termites:

> Termites who spend a year building an average mound 10 feet
> tall have just built, in comparison with their size, the Empire State
> Building. Those who build taller mounds, at nearly 17 feet, have just
> built the Burj Khalifa in Dubai – 2,722 feet and 163 floors of vertigo –
> with no architect and no engineer.[7]

Show me the honey

He could see the honey, he could smell the honey, but he couldn't quite reach the honey.

A A MILNE, *WINNIE-THE-POOH*

I was interested in the building aspect, but rather underwhelmed by the creature itself: termites don't feel very relatable to me. Then I found bees. Maybe it's the honey, which so attracts

Winnie-the-Pooh; maybe it's the fact that they are the most important pollinators of food, and that in 2019 the Earthwatch Institute
declared all bees the most important species on earth.[8] The fact is
that bees increasingly fascinate us, and especially honey bees. I
follow large numbers of beehive keepers on Instagram and bee
blogs and podcasts, and have a large and growing collection of
bee books, bee trivia, bee designs: honey bees have become far
more popular in our imagination than the structural engineering
genius the termite, and they are of course a little fluffier and more
colourful. So bees got to me. I have become friends with the novelist Laline Paull who has written one of the great relatable stories
of creatures – *The Bees*.[9] Margaret Atwood loves it (and you can
see why: it's a sort of *Handmaid's Tale* with honey). The bee society portrayed by Laline is not perfect, and in fact has all the
intrigue, drama, love, violence and daily detail of how bees live as
if it were a human soap opera.

In real life, and indeed in fiction such as *The Bees*, the honeycomb is central to the existence of bees. It is where they live and
work from, storing larvae, pollen and honey. Originally the honeycomb starts with balls of circular wax: circles. But then, for reasons
science has struggled to understand until recently, it hardens into a
different shape entirely: the hexagon. I instinctively knew at that
moment that this was what I had been looking for. The hexagon,
rich in angles and sides, turning out to be so important for the bees
who are in turn so important to us. Added to which is its ability to
both tile and tesselate, so to connect and intersect and form
patterns, and because it also has this unusual symmetry: you can
for instance have half a hexagon, or you can make a three-sided
triangle all within a hexagon. It's the angles of the hexagons, the
edges which all add up to being incredibly strong, practical, useful
and natural. Now that I knew this was the shape and number I
wanted, I began to look not just at the honeycomb but elsewhere
for inspiration. I began to hunt hexagons.

The hexagon turns out, like the number six, to be present in a whole heap of natural settings which can inspire us. So here are six:

1   The planet Saturn, sixth from the sun, features a strange cloud pattern known as 'Saturn's Hexagon', made up of carbon atoms.[10] Carbon is one of the most vital and abundant elements, and while its own shape is not a hexagon, many of the elements it forms into are hexagonal.

2   Take graphene, which is super-light and flexible and roughly 200 times stronger than steel and now being used to revolutionize modern manufacturing. It is derived from graphite, whose hexagonal lattice shape is carbon-based. (Incidentally, graphene was discovered by scientists working at the University of Manchester, a city whose symbol is a worker honey bee.)

3   In the beehive, the honeycomb's cells are designed for maximum space efficiency and oxygen flow – this is the reason that they harden into hexagons and don't stay as squashy circles.

4   Then there is the snowflake. No two snowflakes are the same; they are as individual as we are, and yes, they are all built from hexagon crystals.

5   Right across nature, from the dragonfly's eye to the vast basalt columns such as the Giant's Causeway in Northern Ireland, the hexagon is there, shaping our landscape, our natural world, and so shaping us.

6   Like the number six, once you start to look, hexagons are everywhere.[11] Nuts and bolts, quite literally part of the building blocks in life, are very often shaped like hexagons around the circular hole, for better edge and grip. All modern football design has a mix of 20 hexagons and 12 pentagons which between them make up the perfect aerodynamic ball. And (I promise I am not making this up!) even sex has hexagonal angles now, thanks to a Swedish company called Lelo which

launched a condom range called Hex featuring a lightweight tear-resistant hexagonal structure... I think you get the picture!

The space-efficient, super-strong, tiling properties, the simplicity and symmetry make the hexagon a perfect organizing framework. Just like the number of sides it possesses: the perfect six.

Simplicity's poster-species

As I have already said, while the hexagon is the poster-shape for simplicity, the poster-species is the honey bee.

At first glance, we do not have a lot in common with them, much less so in neurological terms than, say, chimps or even dolphins.[12] The honey bee is miniscule – never more than one and a half inches long (and that's a big variety) and is covered in stripy fur. Oh, and it has two stomachs. So it's not common physical characteristics. But wait. The bee is a 'social insect' which means it has sophisticated communication systems just like us, and research is showing that the pattern of bee 'swarm intelligence' has similarities with neuron activity in our brains, especially when it comes to seeking reward – such as going out and seeking sources of pollen. Research also shows that the process of organizing the society within a hive bizarrely looks a tiny bit like a democratic decision-making process of some kind, based on bee strength, capacity and role.[13] The honey bee gets things done by having very fixed individual roles, but also by performing within a highly organized social system alongside others. In this way it is, like we are, known in biology as a superorganism. Its very productivity comes out of it being a social species. The honey bee is, like ours, an evolved civilization, so that rather than surviving in a fixed state (like a lost, tribe) it survives instead by constantly adapting to its surroundings.[14] Each colony of bees, which can be as large as, say a multinational company or a small community, numbering several tens of thousands, must perform a variety of functions in a coordinated and interconnected way.

This six-legged insect lives and works in the same place, the hive, structured by those hexagon cells which do everything from insulation to storage. Now we all live with a smartphone and the internet, we too live and work in the same place, just like the honey bees.

So that's the theory. What about the practice?

3

From principle to practice

Think in sixes

Hexagon Action puts the Simplicity Principle into practice. Remember that the Simplicity Principle itself focuses on just six words: *keep it simple* and *learn from nature*. Think of Hexagon Action as a six-sided framework for organizing and prioritizing what you do. Use it to help you focus on what matters to you. Productivity comes when we connect with what we want, who we are. It also comes when we clear all the chaotic and complex clutter out of the way. The hexagon is a good shape to use visually but it is also there to remind you of your strength: it is one of the most resilient and strong shapes in nature and it works especially well when it is joined to others.

Simple geometry

One way of applying Hexagon Action is to think in sixes. To limit what you do at any time to six things or the one, two and three things which divide into this mathematically 'perfect' number. The best way to *keep it simple* is to ask how much less you can do, not how much more. Think about how much more working memory you could free up if you did. Another is to think about shape, pattern and process, in a very clear-cut, geometrical way. Hexagon Action lets you *learn from nature* by checking what your own natural resources are and how to best use what you have, from how to conserve your energy to how best to creatively flourish.

Use Hexagon Action as a shorthand in your head. Are you keeping it simple? Are you able to dice and divide up your tasks and challenges, thoughts and feelings so that you can take steps to do what you need to do? I've chosen six sides of simplicity to focus on to help you. Six sides which you need to balance between what is easy and what is hard, and what is simple and what is complicated. Hexagon Action is designed to respect life's unpredictable chaos but to do what you can to withstand it, and to be proactive about taking the steps you can to keep control and focus. The world is big and chaotic but there is pattern, strength and order to be had. Trust me. These six sides are your carbon atoms, the vital building block elements which will keep you strong.

Six simple mantras

Euclid of Alexandria based his theories of geometry on axioms, mini-statements which make obvious sense. So, in a nod to Euclid, each of the sides of Hexagon Action is summarized in a six-word axiom:

1 **CLARITY**. The axiom of Clarity is that '**Being crystal-clear brings you simplicity.**'

   There is nothing worse than muddle, confusion, which brings with it delay, miscommunication, distrust. When you are clear about something you share your Clarity. It is an act of generosity to yourself and to others. Not being clear, on the other hand, badly affects knowledge and the flow of information. The six core elements of Clarity are *Decision*,

Attention, Purpose, Habit, Boundary and what I call *Housekeeping*. The hexagonal shape which speaks most to Clarity for me is the carbon atom, one of the main building blocks of organic life, whose molecular structure is a hexagon-related shape.

2 **INDIVIDUALITY**. The six-word axiom of Individuality is that **'Humans should take priority over machines.'**

We have to work extra-hard in a digital age to know where the human stops and the machine starts, and this brings tremendous anxiety and confusion as well as opportunity. The six-sided elements which help us stay stable and solid in difficult, shifting times are *Identity, Digital Selves, Neurodiversity, Creativity, Integrity* and a keen sense of *Place*. The hexagonal mascot for this side of the hexagon of simplicity is, of course, the snowflake: literally no two snowflakes are ever the same.

3 **RESET**. What six-word axiom best sums up this vital life recipe? **'The always-on mind needs rest.'**

We know a lot about sleep these days, but rest and resetting is not quite the same thing. Part of the epidemic of stress which is sweeping around the world is directly thanks to the 'always-on' culture. The six workarounds I have chosen to highlight are *Release, Mind-less-ness, Curiosity, Nature, Breath* and *Fun*. What hexagonal shape most conjures up Reset? Well, for me it has to be the quilt, that beautiful arts and craft activity which puts the hexagonal shape at the very centre of its pattern for so much of the time.

4 **KNOWLEDGE.** The six-word rule here is that **'Escaping from infobesity must come first.'**

I call how we manage our connections and connectedness in the digital age Social Health. Just like we have learned to manage physical and mental health through diet and exercise, we must now understand that we are in the middle of a digital infobesity epidemic and this brings a whole range of Social Health problems. The six recipes for overcoming infobesity are *Trust, Wisdom, Known Unknowns, Learn, Curate* and *Remember*. Which hexagon best conveys this axiom? It has to be Saturn's Hexagon, the extraordinary and largely unexplained cloud pattern which surrounds the planet Saturn, which lies sixth from the sun.

5   **NETWORKS.** The axiom for this vital element is stark: **'Diverse networks matter more than networking.'**

There is a huge amount to know about how to gain simplicity by focusing on this area alone, because networks underpin everything in nature and in technology. The more we understand, the better we can practise creating rich networks of our own. The six-pack here contains *The Hierarchy of Communication*, *Superorganism*, *Networks*, and the Triple S of *Social Capital*, *Salons* and *Social Six*. What have I chosen as the networks hexagon? It has to be the honeycomb. The bees are the poster-species for simplicity and Hexagon Action. The network of cells inside a honeycomb are always – and I do mean always – made of hexagons. And the hive thrives because of its unique hexagonal cellular system.

6   **TIME.** However we count and calculate, we cannot stretch time. **'Treat your time like your body.'**

This means that what you put in your schedule is as important as what you eat and drink in terms of your Social Health – the way you manage the connected era. Research shows we now spend about six hours a day online.[1] How do we learn to value time and spend it wisely, to control it and make it work for the Simplicity Principle? The six time-related recipes I focus on are: *Deadline*, *Schedule*, *Time Zones*, *Interruption*, *Body Clocks*, and *Past & Present*. The hexagon shape for time is the humble soap bubble. The hexagon is loved in physics because it always seeks to be most efficient for space. When you blow a messy raft of bubbles they too are abiding by the law of physics to be as stable and tight as possible, and become almost perfectly hexagonal. I think of this as a metaphor for how we seek order and efficiency in our lives, despite them being naturally messy too.[2]

PART TWO

Sides of simplicity

The six sides of simplicity on the next pages are a form of 'simplicity slicing', a way of paring down and cutting down. They will help you find your focus and improve productivity because they represent the essence of the values which will carry you through, regardless of how tough or complicated a situation is. Simplicity slicing is about taking small steps in order to get to your whole, better self. It's what Arianna Huffington, founder of Thrive Global, calls 'micro-steps'.

In cooking there is a lot of chopping, slicing and reducing. I want you to 'cook' metaphorically with these six elements, thinking of them as six recipes with six ingredients. Taken together I'm giving you a total of 36 such ingredients which, like any good cook, you will learn to mix and match according to your preference and taste. Right at the end there is a recap: a short Six-Fix of takeaways.

4

Side 1: Clarity

Being crystal-clear brings you simplicity

When I was eight years old, I had one single objective: to own a pair of Wrangler jeans which were all the rage. I could see clearly that the only way to get them was by being super nice to my mother, and I seem to recall that strategy worked. The year was 1972, when Johnny Nash had a huge hit with his song *I Can See Clearly Now*. It played constantly on the radio and has stuck in my mind ever since.

Johnny Nash sang about being able to see 'all obstacles in my way' cutting through the 'dark clouds' of confusion. Something about the message of this feelgood song has always stuck with me, including its optimism that it's going to be sunny from here on in. I realize now that the best way to overcome obstacles is if you can see them clearly, face them clearly, and in turn, be crystal-clear with others.

Clarity is a key element of simplicity, the essential cut-through. Without it you get confusion, delay, dither. I've identified six elements to Clarity which can help us get a clearer, cleaner perspective and help our route to simplicity. If you are in skimming mode, here are the headlines:

1 **Decision:** delay and indecision create unnecessary complexity

2 **Attention:** digital distraction causes poor Social Health

3 **Habit:** pattern and predictability de-clutter choice

4 **Purpose:** productivity comes from purpose and meaning

5 **Boundaries:** setting limits is a vital cut-through

6 **Housekeeping:** discover the joy of filing and tidying

Decision

You don't need more time, you just need to decide.[1]

SETH GODIN

The decision tree

One side of what happens when you are not clear is usually muddle. With that comes stress, anxiety, and often an inability to decide due to so much choice.[2]

I want to focus on indecision which is a big thing for many of us, and the way it can stop us in our tracks. I'm thinking of the delay while someone decides whether to give us a job or not, or how hard it is to take a decision about a job. How sometimes the relatively small daily decision of what to prioritize can get lost in a blur and fog of too many options, too much competing for our attention.

Although we actually make tons of decisions a day unconsciously – it is said that the average brain makes a staggering 35,000 separate decisions[3] daily on everything from where we move our bodies to what to eat and do moment to moment – a surprising number of people I meet feel like they get stuck on deciding, and avoid making decisions if they possibly can. People seem frightened of decisions, somehow. Are you one of them? Don't be.

The ability to decide both faster and more firmly is a sign of Clarity, and therefore of strength. When you decide something it's active and not passive. The ability to decide is the difference between being stuck and moving to a new place. Making decisions is an act of Clarity, clearing the way for other things to happen. Think of a decision as the fruit from a bush, ripe and ready to be plucked. The process which leads to a decision is complex and involves many different parts: like weather, soil, crop strength. In other words, lots of variables which may be well beyond your control (I'm thinking office politics is like weather, with some people blowing hot and cold showers on you the whole time, and so on). But when it comes to *picking* that fruit, there comes a clear moment when that fruit is ready and all you need to do is *decide* to harvest it.

Separating out the indecision – the variables – from the decision, the precise action is an act which reduces complexity to simplicity. A decision moves from being someone else determining your environment and what happens next. You're in charge. You are leading. You're the main actor.

Tyranny of choice

This is not to say that deciding is easy or should be done quickly. But if you value Clarity, you will recognize that making decisions is a cornerstone of achieving it. In psychology the inability to make a decision is called 'aboulomania' (from the Greek meaning 'without will') and is associated with negative emotions, stress and anxiety. The neuroscientist David Eagleman writes in his bestselling book *The Brain* about how we do lots of scenario planning mentally before we make a decision, trying to imagine 'potential futures'.[4]

Marketers almost always present more product and choice as being better than limitation. This is why supermarket aisles, TV channels, brands of beer and make-up are always bursting with more options than we can possibly use. Try searching on Amazon for Post-it notes. The whole point about Post-its is that they are supposed to simplify your physical journey from idea-making to idea-writing: you don't have to put the book you are reading down, you write your note on it, and carry on. Sounds simple. However, Amazon features more than 20 pages of options for buying not just different brands, but differently presented iterations of the same brand. And within each object is something we are all familiar with on Amazon: 'more buying choice'. So, while you can 'buy with one click' you must make a rather complicated set of decisions before you can simply do so.

Decision fatigue

The evidence shows that we actually prefer less choice, not more (sorry, marketers). A famous study in a California supermarket found that a table offering a limited range of six jams elicited a 30 per cent purchase rate, compared to just 3 per cent on the table offering a choice of 24. So, the theory that we like more choice is undercut by a psychological reality.

There is something to be said for limiting decision-making if it gets too much. Barack Obama made the concept of 'decision fatigue' famous when he admitted that he limited his choices of suits and shirts. He told *Vanity Fair* in 2012, 'I'm trying to pare down decisions. I don't want to make decisions about what I'm eating or wearing. Because I have too many other decisions to make.'[5]

Take decision fatigue in other contexts. Like which social media channels to use and scroll through, or which document system to dive into and try to file, or how to start to pick through revision notes or an overfull closet. The process is the same and it's exhausting just listing the endless cluttering of physical and virtual objects we have in our lives today.

Given that life is very, very complex indeed, but that humans want to limit and conserve energy and choice, this could explain why so much of modern 'populism' in politics is about people responding to simple messages rather than complex ones. Take Brexit, and the withdrawal of my country, the United Kingdom, from the European Union. The vote to leave in 2016 was a straightforward proposition: stay or go, and the vote was won on a single, simple message, 'Take back control'.

A politician from the losing side said afterwards: 'We were not clear on the one thing that people wanted to hear.'[6] Simplicity reaches the parts that complexity cannot reach.

There are lots of reasons why we avoid making decisions, and worry about potential futures, or consequences, are clearly amongst them. What if? That's a familiar ringing bell in my head if I am not sure which step to take. What if I... fail? I look ridiculous? The outcome backfires? All of these future scenarios could be true, but one other thing is too: sticking on the ledge of indecision can accumulate more problems than it solves. The base problem doesn't go away, while the imagination runs wild – and a solution still needs to be found.

Then – relief! You make the decision, quickly followed by action, or a sense of resolve. There is something seriously liberating about making a decision – like that moment when you jump off the landing board into the water, or pluck that plum, and the same is true when you pluck up the courage to decide to do something, even if it is hard or brings with it uncertainty. Making the decision can clarify in its simplicity, while not making a decision often extends complexity.

Sitting with a decision

By not making decisions we can often perpetuate complexity. If you're in a position of authority and leadership, a delay can tangle those around you with extra work, extra stress. That's neither fair nor productive. Failure to decide at a certain point is rather like leaving that ripe fruit: two things can happen. Either someone else will pick it, or it will rot. So either a moment is wasted or... someone else could eat your lunch. This does mean that taking too much time to decide is a factor in how clearly you are thinking. Online marketing knows this, as everyone who sees the ticking clock on a hotel booking reservation site knows. If you are unsure whether this is the time to make a fast decision, take six: sit back for six minutes and just *sit with your decision*. Really look hard at it. Do you need to make it? What is holding you back? Then go back to the decision at hand and... make it.

Part of the trick with indecision is to micro-manage it. Instead of thinking 'the consequences of this are enormous and far-ranging' which really ups the ante, try looking at it from a smaller and narrower perspective: 'When I decide this, something particular will change and it will lead to other changes, all of which I can respond to and choose to act on with further decisions.' In other words, if making decisions makes you feel anxious, recognize that and be soothing to yourself, allowing yourself to make smaller micro-acts first. Give yourself six minutes, or six hours if it's a relatively small decision, and perhaps six days if it is a longer one. Spend that time really connecting with what you feel as well as what your choices are and then... pick your fruit. Decision-making can actually be rather delicious!

Having unpacked the value of decision-making, we have the first side of the Hexagon of Clarity. But one of the biggest obstacles to decision-making is something we struggle more and more with in these 'always-on' times and it is why we need to look at it next: Attention.

Attention

The phubbing phenomenon

Have you ever said 'Uh-huh' to someone without looking up from your screen? If so, you have engaged in *phubbing*, the act of snubbing someone while using a mobile phone. You could well be one of the people (I know I am) who picks up your smartphone 80 times a day, or roughly every 12 minutes. That is how often Ofcom, the British telecommunications regulator, says we do.[7] Research also shows that in developed economies we now spend four hours of the day on our smartphones: yep, that's a sixth of the total hours in a day and roughly a third of the hours we are likely to be awake.[8] Before we beat ourselves up too much for that, as if we should just magic up the willpower to be online less, the truth is that the smartphone is increasingly how we communicate, receiving and giving information, being contactable, being social, being at work. This complex computer no bigger than the size of a phrasebook or supermarket cheese makes us all dance on the digital dancefloor much of the time.

And there is a price to pay for it. One aspect is time – and I'll come on to that later in this chapter. But the other is attention itself. Because while you may be forgiven for thinking that you are paying deep attention in these digitally dependent times, head bent over email, news feeds, or social media, lost in thought and clicking endlessly through your attention, your focus is being split like multiple screens, and not in a good way.

The infinite scroll

The clever web designer at Microsoft who came up with the technique known as 'the infinite scroll' of automatic web page refreshing could not have known what a monster he or she had unleashed. We now know that circuitry of the human brain cannot cope with too much distraction or focus-switching. Torkel Klingberg, professor of cognitive neuroscience at the Karolinska Institutet in Sweden, wrote in his book *The Overflowing Brain* that our brains lack 'boundless capacity' to both pay attention and process attention. This is the same conclusion reached in the 1950s by George Miller that the cognitive limit of items we can remember at any given time is around seven (and a major reason why I have focused on six as our working number).

The problem is that we need attention. Attention is what simplifies the complex, weeding out what matters and what does not. Attention is how we prioritize what we do and in what order. Attention is how we use trial and error to reach that all-important decision and make that all-important action. Attention is how we absorb information. Failure to pay attention leads, literally, to accidents, mistakes. In other words, distraction is the result of excessive demands on our attention.

The Stanford University professor Clifford Nass produced some famous research on attention and multitasking and declared people 'suckers for irrelevancy' and that may sound harsh but it is true.[9] Our brain chemistry is actually wired to some degree for distraction, looking for the new, seeking out synaptic connections which are part of what makes human beings wonderfully, well, human. However, when you add the digital overlay on our lives to our natural tendency to wander in our attention, a massive overcomplication occurs, which causes distraction and, for the purposes of Clarity, drains our attention.

When our attention is tied up in the wrong place, dazzled and side-tracked by complexity all sorts of unintended consequences can happen. Out on the street, you may be that person with the headphones on who narrowly avoided being hit by a car because you weren't paying attention. Out in the big wide world other attention problems show up. Take the global financial crash of 2008. In the movie *The Big Short*, with the US government and the credit agencies on Wall Street all hurtling towards financial disaster, sucked under by the complexity of their own instruments which they could no longer understand, one character, an incredulous financial trader, remarks: 'No one is paying attention. It's like two plus two equals fish.' When we are not paying attention, we misread things. When complexity becomes somehow normalized, and everything we do is more complicated than it needs to be, we stop paying attention. We make the wrong assumptions. We think two plus two equals fish.

Twenty-three minutes and fifteen seconds

Two things happen when our brains get distracted. The first is that the brain quickly overloads and in practical terms we slow up, get delayed, losing time as well as attention. Gloria Mark and colleagues at the University of California found that it takes 23 minutes 15 seconds to regain attention and focus after becoming distracted.[10] So even two of those 80 email pickups I mentioned earlier can cost nearly one hour of your time to get properly back on track!

The second problem of inattention is not so much practical – distraction taking you off course – but emotional. Too much overload causes stress and anxiety. The immensely complex nervous system responds to stress by releasing cortisol,[11] and a whole host of physical and mental responses get triggered in our brains alongside a rise in this 'stress hormone' if too much stimulation happens. The over-stimulation of our cerebral cortex, the main part of our brain which processes thinking and organizing our thoughts and information, can trigger anxiety.

Sensory overload is associated with panic, feeling overwhelmed, and triggers a mental shutdown, which can be anything from mild to extreme. All of which draws us away from Clarity and towards muddle, distraction, inattention and feeling wretched. The effects are not unlike those in conditions such as autism or ADHD – only they become prevalent in people who do have an actual permanent genetic predisposition. These are environmental factors and we can do something about this.

You're making me anxious

What nearly two decades of social media has done is bring to the surface just how much connection we crave, but also how isolated it can make us feel. For every person who finds belonging to a special interest group on Facebook an emotional life-saver, someone else may be experiencing bullying or trolling on social media, increasing their sense of isolation. They may be freely giving social media attention, but it might not be doing them any good.

This confusing picture comes from different academic studies which often contradict each other. For instance, a study of young people in the United States published in *The American Journal of Preventive Medicine* showed that young adults who are on social media for more than two hours a day tend to feel twice as lonely, not twice as connected.[12] Yet an important study in the UK by the Royal Society for Public Health had a much more mixed picture.[13] They listed nine potential 'negative effects' but 13 'positive' ones. However, even their research does say that four out of five young adults say that use of social media overall makes their feelings of anxiety worse.

Noticing how much time you spend on social media is a good way of beginning to assess your own levels and how in or out of balance you are. 'Being on' can mean anything from joining purely social sharing and conversations to posting professionally, either on your own behalf or someone else's. But ask yourself this: Can I pick up the phone instead? When was the last time I spoke to anyone in this group? Am I communicating with friends, strangers or a complicated mix of all of these?

A bit of perspective here. Not everyone gets overwhelmed to the point of panic. Not everyone even feels distraction as discomfort by any means. There is often nothing nicer than losing yourself in something: a walk in nature, a good book, an online game, a boxed set... But where shredded attention and distraction really matters is if you have to concentrate to work. That could be school work or undergraduate studies, or it could be income-generating work.

Everyone is working pretty hard to dodge our own inattention. Businesses spend money figuring out how to grab our 'eyeballs' attention, as do governments who want to 'nudge' us into changing our behaviour, and often we forget that unless we work to keep our attention we will lose it. When that happens it isn't just that we lose attention, but that we gain stress.

There is no doubt in my mind that there is a direct connection between the rise in stress and the rise in tech-led complexity. Overload is society's overdose and brings less Clarity just when we need it more. What can be done to minimize stress and regain attention? The first is to recognize the value of unbroken focus. Think of attention as an object you pick up and put down, not something invisible. Think about those 23 minutes and 15 seconds when you task-switch from one thing to another (whether it is from the car to the stove, or the laptop to the meeting) and start to plan where you *put your attention*. Regard attention as something you choose to use, and have a finite amount of, like any *resource*.

Perhaps the most important way to regain and refine your Attention is to see clearly – *with Clarity* – that in order to do so, you need to acquire new Habits.

Habit

The universal language

Habit looks different in many languages: *shuukan* in Japanese; *la costumbre* in Spanish; *l'habitude* in French; *xiguàn* in Mandarin; *die Gewohnheit* in German and *aead* in Arabic, to name just six languages. But it means the same in every language: something which becomes a custom, something which is practised, and it is closely associated with routine.

Cultivating habit is fundamental to simplicity because it cuts down on choice, introduces pattern and therefore reduces the need for too many decisions (even if I have shown you that making decisions can be less hard than you think) and too many distractions. So habit complements Clarity. This makes sense: if every day is a blank sheet this may seem exciting and free from annoying red tape or constraint, but it is jolly hard to keep motivated. All the evidence shows that having some form of routine or habit is fundamental to good mental health.[14] A habit is not the same as a hobby, even though you may enjoy it. A hobby is something you do to switch off, to pass leisure time, to indulge in an interest. A habit is more connected to self-preservation and overall fitness than this: something you do because you know it is a gateway to a clear mind, bringing with it all the benefits of a de-cluttered, simple approach.

I don't personally think having a habit has to be completely rigid. Some people will say it is vital you go to bed and get up at the same time, for instance, or that if you meditate you have to have exactly the same routine. I am a little restless by nature for that and tend to make my habits a bit more elastic! But since I began to explore the benefits of simplicity over complexity, I definitely realized how important it is to have habits, and the difference it makes if I don't.

The 66-day habit

One of the best self-help books ever written (and certainly one of the bestselling) is Stephen R Covey's *The 7 Habits of Highly Effective People*.[15] He says that habit is a mix of *knowledge* (what to, why to), *skills* (how to) and *desire* (want to). Whatever it is, acquiring a new habit or changing an old one is not something instant. Habit takes time and practice. In fact, recent research in the UK showed that it takes 66 days to completely unlearn a habit and start another.[16] You may think that this is an awfully long time – it certainly is longer than it takes to infinitely scroll when on the subway or in a meeting – but the gain if you can stick with it is considerable.

Some of us set habits more easily, but many of us 'fall into' habits. Suddenly we notice that, for good or bad, we have made something a regular part of our routine. The eminent social philosopher Charles Handy had a habit of walking on his local parkland for 40 minutes each morning, to stretch his legs, clear his head and prepare for the day. It became such a fixed routine that the only thing which broke it was a stroke he suffered in his 80s. Charles being Charles, a person full of habit but also of the quality we will see next, Purpose, he merely decided to change his habits to adapt to his more housebound status. Sitting in his house in Putney, south-west London, with the sun streaming through the window, Charles told me that his new habit was to have more of a 'mental walk' – to regain some of his damaged cognitive function in things like memory. He adapted his habits to suit the circumstances. Very practical and not so hard when you put your mind to it.

The good news is that the brain is full of 'plasticity' and rather than being fixed from birth with very little to be done, constantly learns, unlearns and forms new habits, if you let it. Decision can help you set a new habit and replace old ones afresh. The beauty of a new habit is it is a clear marker of change, and a departure from the old to something, often somewhere, new. They say that 'old habits die hard' but remember: mastering new habits makes you feel born again.

Techno-Shabbat

People are now familiar with the idea of a digital Sabbath, but I call mine 'Techno-Shabbat' because it starts at 6.00 pm on a Friday evening, when I come offline, having cleared down my inbox, and connect only with my family and my offline life. This is a ritual and a habit I have built up and whenever I fall off the wagon and stop it my mood becomes anxious and I feel deprived of some kind of psychological safety. My brain is not wired to be permanently firing up by looking at a screen, but neither is my psyche. Although I am not religious, I have learned to appreciate the ritual of regular observance of some kind, based around the family, a meal, some routine. It takes practice, and if you do stop you might need 66 days to get back in the habit, but I find it is so worth it.

The willpower way

A word about willpower. Anyone who has been on a diet or strug-gled to create a new habit with constant temptation knows that there comes a point when willpower crumbles. Entire industries have sprung up trying to make diets more appetizing and easier to follow, and yet, and yet... it is surprisingly easy to fall off the wagon, and emotionally devastating when it comes to this or indeed any kind of other addictive behaviour. So what is going wrong? Are those without willpower lazy or weak? Well, it turns out, no. The truth is that willpower is to some extent, real or imag-ined, experienced as finite, just like a battery or other form of energy.

In a famous experiment conducted in 1998 involving chocolates and radishes of all things, the psychologist Roy Baumeister claimed that if you constantly ask people to override their craving or desire, sooner or later they will run out of willpower, exactly as a car even-tually runs out of gas.[17] This research was updated by the Stanford psychologist Carol Dwek who showed that it may be more our imagined sense of willpower running out which makes us believe it is running out.[18] Either way, willpower exerts a powerful influence and I believe in using it to change how we behave.

These studies certainly revolutionized the way we think about how to limit temptation and change behaviour and are echoed by Richard H Thaler, the 'nudge theory' founder and expert in behav-iour change, and his 'bowl of cashew nuts' experiment at Chicago Booth University.[19] Guess what? If you want to limit snacking, and preserve willpower, move the bowl of cashews away! Both these exercises illustrate something about willpower but they also illumi-nate the value of simplicity. No one is suggesting you have a therapy session to figure out *why* you want the cashews. If you have *decided* not to have them, this simple technique does the trick: it takes on board the neuroscience we now know about willpower and mini-mizes the backlash.

The connection between willpower and habit is important. If you want to start doing something, you can form a new habit partly by minimizing the willpower required to get started. Take exercise: I found that the simple act of always having a gym kit packed transformed the frequency with which I went to the gym. The same was true when I wanted to try some yoga stretches and simple strength-training at home: I created a little corner with a mat and some weights so I no longer had to hunt to locate everything, a sure drain on my willpower. Gone were the endless inner struggles about the idea of any of it, because a very practical step was always taken: bag packed, corner kit ready. It makes a huge difference. The difference between never getting round to it and making it a habit.

Someone else who understands this very well is the writer and broadcaster Tim Ferris. His bestselling book *The 4 Hour Body* was an inspiration to hundreds of thousands of lifetime yo-yo dieters the world over (me included) by pointing out that if you create cut-throughs to the complexity of choice around what food you eat and when, narrowing your decisions in a six-day habit with a seventh 'cheat day', your eating life will be much simpler.[20] He's completely right.

Forming a new habit can involve minimizing distractions – so turning off notifications, or putting away your smartphone entirely for certain periods, for instance. Certainly less is more when it comes to simplicity and Clarity, hence Tim Ferris' limits for a fixed period of time (he addresses the willpower problem by making you exert willpower only for six days: normal diets are infinite and overtax your ability to 'stay strong' in the face of that buffet or that chocolate bar.)

Laying down patterns

Neuroplasticity and our ability to form new habits is obviously mental: it takes place in our minds after all. The temptations of the bread basket are no more 'real' than the digital lure of clicking on your social media when you should be doing something else, as in no one is forcing you. But temptation feels real because it is happening in your head, and in your emotions, and because you have set up habits which take hold really fast. In order to change your habits you have to adjust your thinking. Hexagon Action is a good way to take the stress out of forming new habits to replace and overlay the old ones. There is no point punishing yourself by feeling bad about the behaviours and instincts you have. It's much more productive to look positively instead *towards new habits*. The more you can retrain your mind to welcome your new habits, your Clarity, your decision, and how you are paying attention to creating new ways to be, the less complicated and simpler your task will become.

Let's recap the fundamental principle that simplicity rules over complexity, and that without it we get tugged under the waves of confusion and tangled in the wires way too much. When we deal with things with simplicity, we cut the ties of distraction and favour focus and Clarity. We get more done in limited time. But why bother? This isn't some deeply philosophical question, more of a practical one. What is the point? To answer this is to highlight our fourth aspect to Clarity: Purpose.

Purpose

What gets us up in the morning?

The noun 'purpose' means, according to the dictionary 'the reason for which something is done or created or for which something exists'. That's a pretty huge 'something', wouldn't you agree? In other words, if you have a Purpose, the chances are that you have something which gets you up in the morning. Purpose is in itself a form of Clarity. The upbeat swing in the Johnny Nash tune *I Can See Clearly Now* is very purposeful. There is movement and momentum to Purpose, something forward-marching and meaningful.

Purpose is a word which I associate with a number of positive things. I return again to the dictionary, which tells me that it is 'the reason for which anything is done, created, or exists; a fixed design, outcome, or idea that is the object of an action or other effort'. So a person *has* Purpose. The question is: do you? If so, does this mean you are likely to have more Clarity rather than not, and therefore more ability to cut through the complex and cut to the chase? I believe the answer is another positive: yes. Here's why.

Being purposeful is not to veg out on the sofa or lie inert in a heap waiting for inspiration: not that both of those activities and states are wrong (in fact I think they have a time and place as I will come to when looking at the aspect of Reset). If you have Purpose it immediately conjures up another word for me: energy.

Take Rachael. She is a forty-something single mother of young twin girls living in state-run accommodation in a run-down part of London. One day she realized that a group of aimless teenage boys on the 'estate' were grouping themselves at night in the corridor right outside her daughters' windows, and chatting loudly. The cannabis they were puffing on was drifting through the windows and doorways. Rachael had been aware of the problem of these boys not being occupied and getting increasingly troublesome, but suddenly she saw things clearly. She had to act. That was her Purpose. How she did it was with Clarity. She had to re-route these boys not just to a different physical location, but a different headspace.

Although this social problem is immensely complex – politicians, social scientists, psychologists and a whole range of 'experts' constantly debate the best way to solve stuck problems like this – Rachael kept it simple. She identified local community centres and sources of funding and put the two together. Was it easy? No. Did she ever worry what she was doing? Yes. Did she carry on? She absolutely did. Out of this sprang the London Village Network, one of the most successful grassroots organizations in the capital, which is now recognized as a pioneer of change.

Rachael had Purpose and she kept it simple and clear. In doing so, she also gave her life a meaning she had not realized, because a friend of hers had been in such a gang years before, and had got into serious trouble. That friend had ended up in prison, and after years of neglect and abuse had died after his release. So Rachael's Purpose was personal. It was personified not just in her desire for her children, but for those boys, in memory of her lost friend.

Purpose-built

Do you have Purpose, either in your personal or professional life? Do you have something which matters so much to you, you want to get it done as well as possible, as clearly and as simply? Does what you are doing have a point? Is it worthy of your time, your energy, your skills? Don't be afraid to look clearly at this, because it actually is not that complex. You may not have a lot of choice, because you are on a treadmill to keep bringing in income for your family, or you feel the burden of expectation upon you from others, but the reality is going to be clearer and simpler than you think when you look at it in terms of Purpose.

The corporate world of work has begun to latch on to the idea of Purpose and to give it a boardroom heading, which means in the world of business, it has *arrived*. For business leaders, Purpose means more than profit, it means a reason to produce goods and services which benefit people and planet. In other words, it is a lofty and rather modern aim, brought about in part by consumer pressure and culture change: being a business which just builds skyscrapers and makes money doesn't seem purposeful enough to people any more, as all the research about what Millennials and Generation Z want from the workplace show.

Business has understood that consumers like the idea of Purpose to our products and that they have to embrace sustainability. It's a pretty simple equation: keep customers (and do the right thing too) – probably in that order if we're honest. You only have to look at the way even Coca-Cola, the world's biggest brand, took to addressing the problem of plastic by halving the amount it uses in its products. Increasingly, having Purpose also affects the bottom line of production. Having Purpose keeps you on a clear path and it can drive you to tremendous levels of productivity.

Putting Purpose into practice

Take Maggie O'Kane. When she was a journalist, she won awards. Many of them. British Journalist of the Year; Foreign Correspondent of the Year; Amnesty International Correspondent of the Year; European Journalist of the Year and Irish Red Cross Humanitarian Journalist of the Year. She wrote for *The Guardian*, one of the biggest newspapers in the world.

During her reporting she came across a horrendous crime against girls: a mutilation that happens to a female child once every 11 seconds somewhere in the world: female genital mutilation or FGM. The point about FGM is that in many cultures and countries there is a mistaken belief that this practice is required for religious reasons, when it is not. Maggie reported extensively on FGM and started a campaign within the newspaper: The Global Media Campaign to End FGM. After a thirty-year career in journalism she decided to dedicate her life to working full time on the cause, and spun the project out to be a charity with a simple aim: to reach as many people as possible in Africa to tell them that FGM is not necessary and how to stop it. So far over 800 million people in Africa have received this message. The way in which the Global Media Campaign operates is along Hexagon Action lines. There are three priorities: *i*) they train activists, religious leaders and journalists across Africa to use the media to end FGM; *ii*) the charity supports them to broadcast directly to their own communities, in their own words; *iii*) they identify and bring the most influential religious and political leaders on radio, TV and social media to call for an end to the culture of cutting girls.

When I met Maggie and told her I was writing about simplicity in a complex world she nodded enthusiastically and said me:

> It is unbelievably simple to stop FGM. We found that politicians and the charity/non-governmental organization structures were often bureaucratic and complicated, and more focused on reports to donors than action on the ground. When we look at what is needed it isn't more than the three things we do. We never train more than a handful of people at a time, we always identify less than six influential figures in the community who can have impact, and we just get on with it.

The religious and political leaders are all astonished at the impact and their testimonials bear witness to the effectiveness of the Simplicity Principle in action. Imam Traore, Mali's President of Islam and Population Network said that 'it has achieved more in nine months than we achieved in 25 years' while Dr Tobe Levin, Associate of the Hutchins Center for African American Research at Harvard University, said that 'in more than 40 years the Global Media Campaign's work is the most effective anti-FGM campaign I have ever come across'.

The productivity puzzle

But what about the P-word itself: Productivity? You can't talk about personal or professional Purpose without it. We scratch our heads at the fact that no amount of technology or advanced management seems to improve the overall level of productivity around the world. This suggests that there are unidentified problems which are holding productivity back. Economists call this 'the Productivity Puzzle'.

Those who dislike the idea of measuring people's output at work, especially in manual labour settings argue that it reduces workers to the kind of labourers who worked in early industrial factories in the time of so-called 'Taylorism'. This was in the 1880s and 1890s when machines began to replace humans whose own tasks moved away from being skills-based to repetitive machine-based. Many argue that the same is happening today, with automation and robotics destroying jobs, while others argue the opposite: that employees will have more engaging and productive work to do because robots will do all the boring stuff.

Productivity is definitely linked to Purpose, just as stress in the workplace is linked to toxic management. Why would you be engaged, enthusiastic, productive, if you have no faith in either what you are doing, or who you are doing it for? I think a fundamental aspect of the Simplicity Principle is to *keep it real* and call it out. Productivity is a problem often because Purpose has stopped being clear-cut.

It's worth saying that there is a value in both repetitive tasks and creative ones, but that not every job is both. There is nothing wrong with wanting a job that you just clock in and out of, rather than a more intellectually challenging role, but that doesn't mean you drop the baseline value that every job should be fairly paid and that every human worker should be treated to transparent, honest and supportive employment/hiring practice. There is a connection between the 'toxic workplace' and stress which threatens to engulf the world of work and its profits, and lack of Purpose. Again, I don't think that's complicated. Unhealthy workplaces create ill health. And employer honesty and genuine feeling for their workforce is much more likely to be rewarded with loyalty and productivity.

Companies which do look after their employees and contractors do remarkably well. They don't seem to have anything like the 'productivity puzzle' of others. Take Kronos, the human capital software management business which is based in Massachusetts, USA, but which has 6,000 employees around the world, from India to Australia. The CEO, Aron Ain, describes himself as an 'Un-Leader' and set up a highly innovative system for letting workers set their own holidays and limits. Kronos not only grows year-on-year but is always at the top of any list such as Glassdoor for great places to work.[21] Aron Ain told me something interesting. When they opened in India, which is several hours behind North America, they switched around the working day to accommodate real time for workers on both sides, rather than forcing Indian workers to be up in the middle of the night.

Kronos illustrated something else about Purpose which leads to the next side of the Clarity hexagon: having limits. Even in a high-growth industry, they understand the value of Boundaries.

Boundaries

The difference between successful people and really successful people is that really successful people say no to almost everything.

WARREN BUFFET

How to say No

They say that sorry is the hardest word, but I'm not sure that I agree. I think saying No often is. We know how hard it is to hear it because society is geared fundamentally to Yes: yes you can have it all, do it all, be a success, buy what you want, achieve anything. Yes! Yes!

Of course I believe in the power of saying yes and of thinking what you can do and having Clarity, Purpose, passion is all about that. But remember how finite our attention is (23 minutes and 15 seconds, give or take, is what it takes to get attention *back* after you switch task). Remember too how finite time itself is: the total number of hours in the day is 24 and the fact is that one-third of that time we sleep. So we need to say no and have boundaries whether we like it or not.

Having boundaries is very much what people who have mastered successful simplicity do. People like Warren Buffet, one of the world's richest people and the smartest of investors. His Berkshire

Hathaway company keeps it simple by employing around two dozen employees (although the number of employees in companies he invests in is more like 400,000). He lives simply, spends little, and lives by a mantra that saying no is far more powerful than saying yes.

The meaning of minimalism

Warren Buffet and others are fans of limiting what they take on and say yes to. Their boundaries are consistent with simplicity and with Clarity: it's a kind of minimalism. Warren Buffet is also a big fan of the 80:20 rule, also known as Pareto's Law, which holds that 20 per cent of your effort will result in 80 per cent of your results. In other words, by minimizing the effort you spend on stuff which won't actually make the big difference and focusing instead on the small amount which will really make the difference is a simple and efficient solution.

The design guru from MIT John Maeda also makes this point about minimalism, saying in his neat book *The Laws of Simplicity* that 'thoughtful reduction' is a good strategy, which is a classy way of saying 'less is more'. As he puts it: 'When in doubt, remove. But be careful of what you remove.'[22]

In my case, once I started to look at simplicity as a solution to overload and complexity in my life and that of my businesses, I started to put boundaries in place around everything from who I saw to what I did. Note that I say I put boundaries *in* and not that I took stuff *out*. I wasn't going on an exclusion diet so much as narrowing the focus of what I said yes to, what I prioritized. In practice this meant I reorganized my time, being sure to switch off electronic devices at certain times, and ring-fencing the kind of meetings I had and when those meetings took place. I was pretty staggered by the results. From the moment I started this switch to having better boundaries and focusing on doing less I found that my productivity went up, my mental and physical health improved, and my family and friends saw more and not less of me. Now it's true to say that I'm not as rich as Warren Buffet... but that's down to his simple genius!

But it is worth channelling your inner Warren Buffet on the matter of better boundaries. Decide to take six things out of your schedule right now that, if you are honest, you can do without: a meeting you can delegate to others; a period of time better spent thinking and reading rather than being buried in emails. Then use the other elements of Clarity to sharpen your senses; pay close attention to what you are feeling, what your sense of Purpose is, whether you have got some bad habits cluttering up your 'yes' side of the scorecard; and go on a little slimming exercise. Incidentally, Warren Buffet also goes for minimalism: he doesn't have a smartphone and limits what he eats each day. So he's applying nearly all the principles of Clarity in everything he does – and with it the Simplicity Principle.

Counting it out

One good way to keep track of your boundaries is to measure them. I used to be a bit too relaxed about measurement, thinking it was for control freaks. I never used to weigh myself, or count steps, or record what I actually did in the hours of a day. I found that one thing thrived when I did this: the art of frittering away time and losing a grip on my attention and Purpose. I have become a convert to some form of measurement, even though I am still not convinced that you need fancy measurement (like app-controlled devices to record your walking). What I have become a fan of is using measurement as a way of owning choice, decision, intention, Purpose, and of helping me decide what habits to form and what my clear priorities are.

I have begun to embrace measurement as a meaningful boundary line, no different to knowing to keep on the right side of the road.

But remember that the point of measurement is to deliver Clarity and not spawn complexity. I'm highly critical of the '360 degree' appraisal system inside corporate culture for instance. This is where everyone is encouraged to give their personal opinion of everyone else for candid feedback, which is then fed into some kind of human and electronic algorithm to decide on promotion and pay rises. I know: many human resource managers will hate me for saying this, but it's true. Quite apart from the invitation to be overly critical and to settle scores which this kind of system encourages, it also creates complexity which is totally 'extra'. A far simpler system is to lay out clearly what is required of people inside a team or a company, to give them the right management, leadership, incentives and structure, and let them get on with doing their jobs.

So please: by all means measure, but keep it clear and simple. Don't go overboard!

Governments tend to be good at measuring because they have to account for the way public money is spent. Thanks to new understanding of psychology and the rise on 'behavioural economics' they are able to use new tactics and measure the responses. In Chile the government decided to make their electricity bills clearer and simpler, after receiving 30,000 complaints relating to 34 different electricity providers. By undertaking a detailed set of micro-adjustments to their policy, their new-styled electricity bills were changed to be far simpler and as a result scored over 50 per cent in consumer confidence in understanding the bills, with almost double the level of understanding compared to before.[23]

What does success look like?

I learned the best way to measure success when I was a young book publicist. I had a really good record of placing articles in the press, I got on well with authors, and made the leap from being in-house to setting up my own publicity agency with a single contract from my old boss, a legendary life force of an Australian publisher and writer called Carmen Callil. This meant I was being paid from specific budgets for specific books, and my clients really wanted to know what the ROI – or return on investment – would be. This is easier said than done with publicity when often the time and labour goes into pitching, with no control over the result, unlike, say advertising where at least you can buy it.

I recall an impressively scary meeting with the boss of one particular publishing house. Nellie Flexner was a supersmart no-nonsense American who had a brilliant track record in her campaigns. Outsourcing books to external publicists was something she did rarely, but on this occasion, it was the autobiography of the most famous sports manager in Britain at the time, the English football team coach, Terry Venables. He was contractually obliged to do certain publicity events which meant the publisher was under pressure to line up some strong media opportunities and keep him and his agent both happy and on their toes. So when she asked to see me before giving me the contract, I knew she meant business. 'I have only one simple question for you,' Nellie said, fixing me with her friendly but intense gaze. 'What does success look like?' She was asking me to name what the measurement was – was it column inches (this was pre-internet) or was it the *kind of outlets*? We ended up having a really interesting discussion about strategy and I left the meeting determined to earn her investment and her approval. The measurement, it turned out, was a combination of dealing with the media and the author and his agent, which turned out to be pretty tricky. Asking myself the simple question 'What does success look like?' has become one of my go-to ways of getting Clarity if I am ever drowning in too much complexity.

There just remains one final side to Clarity and the role it can play in bringing simplicity to your life. It is something which is both an attitude and an action. It stays close to where you live, very close. For this reason I call it Housekeeping.

Housekeeping

There should be a place for everything, and everything in its place.
MRS BEETON'S BOOK OF HOUSEHOLD MANAGEMENT

Recipe for success

A hundred and fifty years ago, back when we all still lived without electricity, cars, aeroplanes and when clouds were the kind you see in the sky and not relating to computers (which had not yet been invented) an Englishwoman was writing very modern and up-to-the-minute advice on cooking, cleaning, and maintaining order in your home. Isabella Mary Beeton wrote about recipes, household affairs and a set of values about how to live, first in instalments in *The Englishwoman's Domestic Magazine* and then in book form. It was an instant bestseller, selling 60,000 copies within a year and over a million copies within a decade. It was called *Mrs Beeton's Book of Household Management* and has set a benchmark for cookery writers and lifestyle gurus ever since.

Mrs Beeton was the 19th-century version of Marie Kondo, the Japanese author and TV presenter whose *Life-Changing Magic of Tidying* has sold well over three million copies around the world. Both of them have simple, straightforward messages which focus on keeping Clarity, neatness and order where it matters most: your home.

There is no doubt that if you have a system and a simplicity in your home you can carry that out into the world. This is not a rallying cry for matching minimalism everywhere, or for making every home look like a hotel room (although the trend for hotels is very much to try and look like homes these days), but it is to say that if you can't have Clarity about where things belong and where to find them, and if everything is jumbled and messy, the spillover is likely to go outside your front door.

I actually don't just mean the home and where you live when I talk about housekeeping, not least because so many of us work and live in the same places, or a mix of places. With the decline of full-time employment and the office as a place where you spend your career or even the majority of your working week, and the evidence that as many as 80 per cent of us will be making our own luck as freelancers in the gig economy by 2030, housekeeping is a state of mind and a strategy as much as it is a location.[24] The priority is to notice what makes this 'situation' muddled and how to clear it up.

The guru who first got me interested in this kind of attitude was the author David Allen, whose book *Getting Things Done* is permanently within reach on my bookshelf.[25] What David Allen, Isabella Beeton and Marie Kondo have in common is that they see Clarity as clarifying, and simplicity as liberating. As do I.

Clutter

In the United States there are over 50,000 self-storage facilities, covering nearly 40 billion square feet of space. Europe has over 10 million square feet of storage space, with the average letting taking up nearly 4,000 square feet, while Singapore's largest self-storage business, Storhub, was sold to investors at a value of $180 million. Storage is a growth market to be in.[26,27] The biggest growth in self-storage is not business, which is if anything downsizing, giving employees laptops and holding data in the cloud, but in personal storage. What do people store? Clutter. Overflow. Stuff. Things they hold on to when they need to let go. James Wallman wrote a brilliant book, *Stuffocation*, about how we are consuming more and more things at the expense of memories and experiences and he's right.[28] More stuff is a form of complexity. There is an old saying, 'out of sight, out of mind', and unfortunately, it's true. Can you honestly say you know what is in the attic, under the bed, or in your own storage facility? It's one thing to try and organize things *away* and order storage: at least that is an attempt to limit overtaxing your sightline and space. But it isn't nearly far enough if you want Clarity of thought, Purpose, decision, attention, and fresh habits. Yet again, brain chemistry proves this point.

In our brains, just behind our foreheads there is an area called the dorsolateral prefrontal cortex, which controls both decision-making and emotions. Research done by the Centre for Applied Research in Decision Making shows that it's like a circuit-breaker: overload it with too much stimulation, too many requests to make decisions and we cut out.[29] That's a plain and simple response to complexity: our brains just shut it out. Think what this means in practice: all those *important* things we may overlook, because our heads are so stuffed with the wrong things! Many of us worry about Alzheimer's and dementia and biochemical causes of memory loss, but stress and anxiety and overload are also causes of similar symptoms, which are called 'pseudodementia' by psychiatrists. The good news is that de-cluttering can actually free up headspace as well as brainspace, and arguably reverse some of these symptoms.

Someone who is also interested in organization, behaviour and managing modern complexity is author Derek Draper. He is a highly successful business psychologist and consultant and the author of a great book called *Create Space*. I went to talk to him in his spacious home in London which he shares with his wife, the national TV presenter and broadcaster Kate Garroway. I went on a Wednesday, which is the day of the week Derek ring-fences for time to think, write and be away from the clutter of a commute or meetings. (Very sensible.) Derek showed me a tiny box-room not even big enough for a bed, in which he keeps a low chair and a poster fixed on to the sloping roof wall. 'This room is essential to me for two reasons,' Derek told me. 'Firstly, I separate out thinking from doing, so this is not my office, which is stacked with papers and a computer. And secondly, this is a space which my wife, who is very comfortable with chaos, clutter and clothes, is banned from.'

Your inner housekeeper

It took me years to realize that a particular piece of David Allen's advice rings true in my head almost every day. This is it:

> Most people feel best about their work the week before their vacation, but it's not because of the vacation itself. What do you do the last week before you leave on a big trip? You clean up, close up, clarify, and renegotiate all your agreements with yourself and others. I just suggest that you do this weekly instead of yearly.

Of course! Clarity is continuous, not just for vacations. If I do manage to keep to this rule, I definitely achieve more and feel less ground down. I feel lighter and more purposeful. It's simple common sense, after all.

There is something else David Allen advocates, which is that you need to have one place for everything, so you can always find it. This piece of advice is also as simple as it is effective. I cannot recommend too highly investing in drawers or files or folders or just piles which you dedicate to one thing: household appliance documents, or contracts, or medical information, instead of scattering it everywhere. Because not doing it, and scattering things chaotically or randomly instead creates clutter, not Clarity. Not only can it be terrifying to find something in an emergency when you don't know where to begin, but it symbolizes something deeper: if you can't keep house well, what else is too messy in your life?

When I am working, if I just abandon myself to whatever flies into the inbox, if I am at the mercy of a schedule made by someone else, or if I have way too much to do given the hours in the day, I'm anything but relaxed and perhaps more importantly, I'm wildly unproductive. My head crowds with the complexity and jumps from task to task. I get distracted, agitated, tired. I tend to drink coffee and then I'm also wired. If I lack Clarity, focus, Purpose, and do not have my internal 'house' in order, it's chaos.

The people I admire greatly in life when I watch them work are hotel housekeepers and cleaners. The margins in the hotel business can be tight and housekeeping takes time. Good hotel chains have it down to a fine art, knowing exactly how long it takes to tuck in a bed cover, clear out a bathroom of a particular size. What you notice if you watch hotel housekeeping in action out of the corner of your eye is that it is based around doing one thing at a time, in a particular order: monotasking. Hexagon Action is not about doing six things at once, even if you work in a pattern and a sequence. I wish we would apply housekeeping logic more to what we do. We should also take note of research coming out of Stanford University that multitasking is nothing short of a myth, really.[30] This shows that when we do try to do more than one thing at once it has an immediate and negative impact on our memory.

When you adopt the Simplicity Principle, your own mind clears. When you keep your mind and your surroundings tidy – both literally and metaphorically, because you too have a *system*, everything will de-clutter. You will feel better about even the most trying circumstances. Those circumstances are of course individual to you.

SIX
FIX

CLARITY

1 **Prevent decision fatigue.** Keep your decisions down, make them by using Hexagon Action to really home in on your choices.

2 **Pay attention to attention!** The more you scroll, the more you lose those 23 minutes and 15 seconds it takes to get your attention back. Avoid the infinite scroll.

3 **Take a Techno-Shabbat.** Find a time when you get physical not digital, and make that day or even part of a day your 'Techno-Shabbat'. Look at all your rituals and embrace habit, even if you start one to break another.

4 **Puzzle your productivity.** Are you being productive? If not, why not? Could Purpose be the key?

5 **Just say No.** Choose what you say yes to and don't be afraid to say no. Boundaries are good!

6 **Cultivate a tidy mind.** De-clutter surroundings, even if that means rearranging the mess you like: but be clear what your process is to find something when you need it.

5

Side 2: Individuality

Humans should take priority over machines

Simplicity is the keynote of all true elegance.

COCO CHANEL

Individuality stands out. It is quite singular, separate from the rest. Charismatic leaders have Individuality. Landmark buildings have it: it's what makes them landmark in the first place. Companies which stand the test of time because they adapt but stay distinct from the competition have it (we still don't know the *exact* Coca-Cola recipe, do we?). Individuality has a simplicity about it: it stands out and stands apart. Individuality also has a timeless quality. The fashion house Chanel, standing for elegance, style, simplicity, has been around since 1909. To be a privately-held business for over 100 years is remarkable. To be in the fashion business for that length of time is pretty stunning. Simplicity runs like a thread through Individuality.

It is a mistake to think you have to work hard at Individuality. If anything, people work too hard at it, and make it much more complicated than it needs to be. I think you just need to notice and nurture it, which requires much less energy and mystique. Some of the great individuals of our times may have worked incredibly hard to succeed, but their Individuality was something they accepted as a given. Did David Bowie toil away trying to be different, or was he singular in the first place? How about the Japanese novelist Haruki Murakami? His work has been translated into 50 languages, selling millions around the world. I adore his pared-down prose, his quirky characters. There is no one who writes quite like him. His voice is distinct, even in translation. What about the pioneering female Olympic champion Derartu Tulu? This long-distance runner became the first black African woman to win an Olympic gold medal, at the Barcelona Games in 1992. She had raw talent, drive and unique capability. How did a young girl in an all-male society in rural Ethiopia outrun her male counterparts and, with no training or money behind her, become a national and international star?

Whatever it is, star talent cannot be made by artificial intelligence. Our Individuality is what keeps us safe from the rise of the robots, even if, as we shall see later in this chapter, the power of humans working *with* machines can be a simple and powerful solution to some problems. The more we connect to our Individuality, who we are as simple *people*, without a computer in sight, the better. Even if we have quieter talent than superstars, it doesn't matter or make us less individual. All too often we get blown off course into complicated places we don't want to be – the wrong job, the wrong relationship, the wrong situation – when we disconnect from this fact. Trusting our Individuality and building on that is both simple and powerful.

In this chapter, there's a hexagon to help you connect to what makes us all tick. Think of the six ideas as spokes within a wheel which you can turn and stop when you like. They can be taken together, or separately:

1 **Identity:** knowing who you are is powerfully effective
2 **The Digital Self:** be on- and offline for Social Health
3 **Neurodiversity:** recognizing the talent within all of us
4 **Creativity:** the way to let Individuality thrive
5 **Integrity:** how to keep honest and true
6 **Place:** location, location, location is key

Identity

I am no bird; and no net ensnares me: I am a free human being with an independent will.

CHARLOTTE BRONTË, *JANE EYRE*

The human snowflake

Here's a hexagon for you: the snowflake. You might not know that there are, literally, infinite varieties of this gentle, fluttering mixture of falling ice crystals which always form into hexagonal structures.

What are snowflakes exactly? Why is every single one unique? According to the US National Oceanic and Atmospheric Administration it is because:

> they all follow slightly different paths from the sky to the ground – and thus encounter slightly different atmospheric conditions along the way. Therefore, they all tend to look unique, resembling everything from prisms and needles to the familiar lacy pattern.[1]

Humans are as infinite as snowflakes. Indeed, we all follow slightly different paths, encountering our own 'different atmospheric conditions' along the way. I don't know whether I would identity as a 'prism person' but I know that when I describe someone as being 'prickly' or 'delicate' I could be describing someone, not a snowflake. We talk about 'the Snowflake Generation' which has become shorthand for Millennials and Gen Zs who take offence at the slightest thing, but the truth is we are all in a way Generation Snowflake, and not in a bad way: because we are as individual and as diverse as the real thing.

Remember that I don't think you can eliminate complexity, just because you're aiming for simplicity. Not much is more complex than personality combined with circumstance. We are knee-deep in our own quirky Individuality and those of others, and we have to duck and dive constantly, a complex task. But how we behave can be streamlined and simplified, as we understand more about ourselves and our choices.

But back to Individuality itself for a moment, in all its infinite glory. Sport is a good way to understand how out of a group, with all of its diversity, comes a single, simple, standout winner. There is always something magical about an Olympic Games opening ceremony: each team parades through the stadium doing something identical in one way and wholly individual in another. They all bear national flags, and they all keep to the choreography they have learned which is as much for the TV cameras as anything else. But they all look different. They dress differently. They behave differently. And when they play in the games, it is their difference, not their similarity which allows them to stand out and to win. My favourite Olympic sport is gymnastics. Because even though the gymnasts are part of a team, you watch them as individuals. The greatest gymnast this century has to be the American Simone Biles, who surpasses every single kind of record or even type of movement with her originality and flair. Watching Simone Biles move is almost like watching a floating object rather than a person. But of course, she is just like the rest of us in many ways, just with superhuman talent and levels of dedication to honing her skills. Simone Biles' identity is singular and yet collective. We know she is on a pedestal and yet we can rightly claim her as one of us on terms we too may identify with – as a woman, an American, an African American, a member of our human family.

The Blended Self

The more we discover about personality and identity the more we realize it is less fixed and more of a dissolve (rather like a snow-flake) between different modes, pretty much all the time. The distinguished psychology professor Brian Little has discovered that we all possess 'Free Traits',[2] which means that even if you are, say, an introvert, you can in fact choose to make yourself do something extrovert if you have the right motivation.[3]

Our individual personalities revolve and change. They are mobile. We used to have far more static and fixed roles in life, as we tended to stay in one place, living within one community. Today we are on the move, both in terms of our jobs and our lives, more than ever before. We can now expect to live until 100, and change jobs at least as many times as a hexagon has sides. As our roles have changed, and the idea of a place of work, so has the identity of who we are as a person with a working life and a home life changed. I call this new identity 'The Blended Self'.

I first coined this phrase in my book *Fully Connected* to identify the person whose life is not only strictly personal ('stay-at-home-mom') or professional ('office worker') any more, but increasingly a blur and blend of both. We may retire from one job and have a series of side hustles for others. We may work flexibly out of some-one's office in one country and move somewhere else entirely and take our work with us, virtually. Our lives are no longer fixed, nor are the places we lead those lives. They no longer have the simplic-ity of a monotask but the complexity of a multitask. But they can have the Simplicity Principle applied to them, to keep us on track, based on our individual Blended Self.

Acknowledging your Blended Self doesn't have to be complicated: it can be viewed as a series of simple identities which overlap. There is a wonderful film made in the early 1980s called *Local Hero*, about a US oil company executive sent to a remote Scottish village to try and buy the surrounding land, only to fall in love with the community.

As much as anything this is a story about our roles in life and how they are never fixed, such as the hot-shot executive who realizes he has his priorities wrong. But it also sheds light on the multiple roles individuals have to play in small tight-knit communities. There's a brilliant scene when the American finds himself being served a drink from behind the bar of the pub by the accountant with whom the hot-shot is negotiating. He shrugs at the surprised American, and keeps on pulling the pint anyway. *Local Hero* is, of course, a film which pays homage to simplicity, and to simpler times.

The Digital Self

Identity theft

One so-called simpler time (although every era seems fiendishly complicated compared to the one before) was pre-internet. Not that we want to be without it, but let's be honest, it is everything from a time-suck to a vortex of limitlessness. In practical, daily terms one of the most complex things we face is the constant zigzagging between human real time, real-world situations, and whatever we need to do online. It feels so normal for everyone to cross the digital dancefloor many times on a daily basis that we don't think about it. The Digital Self is almost like a new species who needs to be studied in order to be better understood. Who is this person? In fact, it's plural: the average social media user (well over half the people on the planet use social media) don't just have one 'handle' with which they login, but several.

More than this, back in simple internet times, less than a single human generation ago, you perhaps only had Facebook. I recall using Facebook for the first time and it was fairly simple. It didn't have news feeds, it didn't have groups, it didn't have 'like' buttons, it just had posts and looking up people to invite them to be friends. But almost immediately, things got complicated. Big Data got in the way and the algorithms got busy and the bias got heavy and before you knew it, simply grouping your friends online got complicated. I happened to be in California at a conference at Facebook when it turned 15, and realized that in that time the number of social media accounts the average person has had doubled every two years. It now exceeds Hexagon Action and is on the cognitive limit of seven. That's seven different social media accounts for one single person. Not at all simple.

Then there's the time it all takes. We've already seen that we check our smartphones up to 80 times a day.[4] This includes coming online to check email or retrieve a document, or participating in a group chat, or doing some online shopping, or gaming, or any one of at least 10 distinct activities we can all now do if we are anywhere near a connected device (which is at least four too many for Hexagon Thinkers). According to Digital Data World research, we are on the internet for over a third of all the waking time in our lives. Or, guess what, Hexagon Thinkers: six hours a day.[5]

Whatever else we are doing digitally, it involves some form of identity. In fact, the number one cause of fraud for business globally is identity theft.[6] But it isn't just criminals playing with who we are online. It is us, robbing ourselves of who we really are in order to be someone else, online. This can all too easily blunt your sense of identity and rob you of your all-important Individuality. It becomes easy to mentally merge in your mind who you are and how you value yourself with how others see you through this almost-you identity online: filtered through your device, your Instagram or Twitter handle, your group chat name, your followers, your posts' likes and shares, the comments underneath your posts.

Decision exhaustion

I wrote earlier about online-related anxiety. It isn't just the pressure to keep up appearances and give the impression of being happy and successful, although that is clearly having a major negative impact, especially on vulnerable teenagers. There has been a significant uptick in suicide amongst young women in particular since the advent of social media, and a significant amount of research showing that those people predisposed to depression are likely to have their negative self-image reinforced, not repaired, through excessive use of social media.[7]

No, it's more than this. It's the infinite complexity of choice. Remember decision fatigue and Barack Obama's decision to limit his clothes to a set group, to eliminate stressful, time-sucking choice? Social media takes this problem to a whole new level. It's more like decision exhaustion. Which channel? What comment? Who to follow? How to respond? What to post?

I am not one of the doomsayers who believes that social media corrupts us or makes us commit suicide – I think there are many complex factors and to try and be simple for its own sake risks being simplistic, which I have said before is not the same thing. But that doesn't mean that being yourself online is in fact the same as being yourself offline and in person. This is like saying that a person under the influence of alcohol or drugs is the same. The experience exaggerates or alters personality. Researchers looked into trolls on social media on Reddit in a new experiment around what's called restorative justice – putting perpetrators directly in touch with their victims. In one case, one reaction was this: 'Dang this wasn't the context that I remembered,' he types at one point, after looking at past bullying posts. 'I thought someone else was the instigator and I felt ganged-up on or something. But… looks like I was the instigator.'[8]

On-off switching

There clearly has to be a way to limit our digital selves being mistaken for our full selves, and one of the answers has to be to limit our use of online media when we want to communicate something. What that means, simply, is coming offline in a purposeful way. I don't think it is any different to putting your computer to sleep, or even putting yourself to sleep: you have to *switch off* sometimes.

We have become so addicted to technology that we have imagined that it is normal to binge addictively, but we would not eat or drink or do anything to such excess and not expect consequences.

The problem with being connected to a digital device when you communicate is greater than just being online for other purposes. This isn't really about the screen, so much as the screen *presence*. Interestingly, email is in some ways the least-worst offender, although it gets much of the bad press. While there clearly is a problem with a culture where we email someone we are sitting next to (highly normal if ridiculous!) or just over-emailing (if anyone still uses 'Reply all' please put them in a cupboard until they sort themselves out: it clutters up everyone else's inbox and is absolutely *not* in the spirit of the Simplicity Principle!) the real culprit isn't the communication platform itself.

No, the problem isn't email versus WhatsApp, or Slack versus Messenger. The issue is how real you are when you communicate, whether you bring yourself to the exchange, when the risk is that the electronic identity is a barrier, a separation which stops a real connection taking place at all. If this is happening you know it won't make the outcome simple or straightforward, but confusing. In fact, if you made a point of standing up six more times a day and walking across to speak to someone to tell them what you wanted, or picking up the telephone to them, you'd almost certainly find six times less confusion or 'miscom' as a result. Try it. You know it makes sense.

Neurodiversity

S is for sensitive

In order to try and pin down personality, psychologists have famously classified five different personality types, dubbed OCEAN: Openness, Conscientiousness, Extroversion, Agreeableness, Neuroticism.[9] I'm going to add a sixth one, for Hexagon Action's sake: Snowflakery. Let it stand for Individuality and the blend between all the other aspects of personality. Let it also stand for Neurodiversity, and the relatively new way to describe both 'neurological' and 'diversity'. But I'll start first with an obvious aspect of Snowflakery, made famous by the Snowflake Generation: Sensitivity.

There is absolutely nothing wrong with being sensitive when it means being connected to your feelings. Often, a sign of deepening depression and stress is a feeling of being de-sensitized and disconnected. It is a form of misguided self-protection: trying *not* to be sensitive, because it is too painful. Being in favour of sensitivity is not an argument in favour of politically correct 'wokeness' which is what the Snowflake Generation is taken to stand for. You know, taking offence at everything and feeling triggered by things which older generations just call life. No, I'm talking about a different meaning of 'sensitive', one which is tuned in, *aware* of what's going on for you and how this affects your core personality. It is not based on politics or belief about the world, it's based on one simple thing: you in this situation.

Being sensitive to your inner, private snowflake is an essential survival technique and it hinges on a simple connection to feelings. I once benefitted hugely from some therapy when I was feeling so sensitive to everything I thought I would actually dissolve and disappear. Over time with what I like to call 'assisted self-help', I learned that having your feelings is not the same as being consumed indefinitely and irretrievably by them. I learned that it is the feelings which will dissolve, like snowflakes, not the person. I became more sensitive, not less, and I found that it calmed and grounded me: I started late (I was over 40), and it took a good few years (I made quite a dent on that shrink's couch) but suddenly sensitivity felt simple and my life a whole lot less complex.

These days, if I start to feel emotionally fragile, overly sensitive, the first thing I do is try and understand what the feeling is. I have come to recognize my inner snowflake as a very healthy early warning system: something isn't right and I need to find out what it is in order to act and react. The feelings themselves may be complicated – usually unhappiness and stress are a mix of noisy, messy, rather infinite and imprecise discomforts aren't they? However, when I stop what I am doing, stop fidgeting, distracting, diving into the drama of the moment (the trigger can be someone else throwing down their snowflakes), when I do that, things start to simplify. It's rare that I can ever count more than one or two things which are actually the problem when I focus on asking myself what's wrong. In other words, even when I am feeling very complicated and tough things, I can apply the Simplicity Principle to them. I can unpick and unpack them. I can count them. I can identify them and in doing so reconnect with my own identity: who I am and what I feel. It's a really powerful feeling.

Now let's come to Neurodiversity. As Temple Grandin and Richard Panek say:

> What would happen if the autism gene was eliminated from the gene pool? You would have a bunch of people standing around in a cave, chatting and socializing and not getting anything done.[10]

Groupthink

One-size-fits-all may be good for some things: carry-on luggage limits, cartons of juice, prescription medication, but less so people. I think it is a shame that we have created a society which puts 'norms' above all else. It is encouraging that we now can talk about 'neurodiversity' and begin the green shoots of recognizing true Individuality, but my goodness it has taken time. So many systems and structures remain fixed, geared towards a narrow definition of what it means to be individual and singular, rather than a generous and broad one.

The simple fact is that a person whose skills are different from the norm can be the make-or-break addition to a project or team. If we are applying a little Hexagon Action to the idea of Individuality, then a wholly unique snowflake of a person in your organization is exactly what you need: even if you have to break an old pattern of thinking and doing to realize it.

In social psychology and the science of behaviour 'Groupthink' is irrational decision-making between a group of people at the expense of Individuality and common sense. In other words, everyone is expected to conform to a norm and anyone who doesn't is regarded as, well not normal, and to some degree, inferior. At the very least Groupthink is simplistic rather than simple. By which I mean, it assumes that there is such as think as a normal group who *should* be and act the same, rather than a more simple reality: people are different.

It is so important to stress that simplisticness is not our friend here: the Simplicity Principle respects complex situations and comes up with individual workarounds: it is a really important distinction.

This is different from the fact – which I'll come on to shortly in the section on Networks – that tremendous things can happen when we behave collectively and as a group. But all collective activity starts from individuals with distinct social qualities and skills. The same goes for social insects like bees and it certainly goes for people. In other words: neurodiverse people are just the special individuals who stand out.

The Chief Happiness Officer

There is a wonderful non-profit organization in the UK called Team Domenica[11] set up by the mother of a charismatic young woman born with Down's Syndrome. Domenica Lawson, now in her twenties, is the niece of the TV chef Nigella Lawson and was Princess Diana's last godchild. The first time the world saw Domenica she was photographed alongside Diana at her christening in the arms of her mother, the campaigner Rosa Monckton. But Domenica did not have an easy or a blessed life. Opportunities for people with conditions such as Down's Syndrome don't improve if you have rich and famous relatives or know royalty. Domenica's mother, who campaigned tirelessly for better opportunities to help her daughter become an independent adult, realized that she had to do something herself. She also realized that the key to independence is – of course – employment, not just for the income, but for self-respect. Rosa says that Team Domenica's mission is 'to help people with learning disabilities discover their career potential, to create employment opportunities and to remove barriers to work in local communities.' Domenica was 24 years old when she proudly showed off her first paycheque for working in the Brighton Pavilion Café. She told *The Sun* in the UK that 'it feels amazing really and I feel very important to have money'.[12]

The workplace, as well as general society, has been slow on the uptake when it comes to recognizing that difference doesn't mean less or wrong. The father of John Cronin, a young American with Down's Syndrome, was so convinced that there was a role for John in business that together they set up John's Crazy Socks,[13] designed specifically to harness John's gift for communicating and his attention to detail and his sense of fun. John, who is his company's 'Chief Happiness Officer' became the first person with Down's Syndrome to win a major business award, the EY Entrepreneur of the Year award. The business turns over in excess of $5 million a year.

Then there's another source of happiness: the entrepreneur who takes risks on neurodiversity itself. Brian Jacobs, a venture capitalist, spent 30 years in finance before starting a new venture dedicated entirely to backing businesses which invest in employees with autism.[14] He invested $10 million of his own money. In the business of impact investing, companies benefitting from his investments like Auticon, an IT company, backs employees who bring 'sustained concentration and perseverance when tasks are repetitive', as just one example.

The way through life's infinite and troubling complexity is to carve out individual, simple, straightforward paths, which you can only do on a personalized basis. It is not even that no two people are the same. No two organizations are. The more we adopt and embrace a truly snowflake approach – that is to recognize our Individuality, to truly see it – the more chance we will have to get things right. Instead of thinking of difference as a problem, let's look at how it can work for and with us.

How we express our Individuality and identity is part of the magic of being human. It stands us apart from the machines. The absolute epicentre of this Individuality is our Creativity.

Creativity

Creativity is not just for artists. It's for businesspeople looking for a new way to close the sale; it's for engineers trying to solve a problem... Creativity is a habit, and the best creativity is the result of good work habits.[15]

TWYLA THARP

Creative juices

When you do something creative, you form a deep connection. In music, poetry, art, dance and the obviously creative industries, connection is the currency you want. Elton John and Bernie Taupin are two of the legendary singer–songwriter creative forces in modern pop: each and every song in their back catalogue of 30 albums cuts simply through to that place inside their fans where they feel seen, understood. When I listen to a piece of music which stirs something deep within me – it could be a pop song or a Beethoven piano sonata – I am moved. Nothing complicated. I have certainty in that moment. One of the great pleasures in life is knowing what does move you creatively. You have to tap into and connect with your own Individuality to discover it if you are not lucky enough to just *know*. It took me many years to know what visual creativity I liked, when I instinctively understood how much music and words affected me. I had no problem during childhood onwards liking choral and popular music, musicals and novels, but I always felt pretty disconnected from appreciating art. Then as a teenager I discovered the simplicity of the Belgian surrealist painter Magritte and suddenly I got it. I adore his paintings of perfectly drawn impossible things: mountains made to look like eagles, and men floating through the sky in bowler hats, colours and scapes which touch me very deeply. The connection I feel to that art is very simple and yet very, very complex too. I can hardly put it into words. That's creativity.

Of course, the creativity which moves me is not the one which moves you. That's Individuality for you. The beauty of belonging to a social species is when you are all united by something special, something connects the whole group. But what is it about creativity which is both individual but also simple?

Don Bledsoe, the founder of a scriptwriting consultancy, Script Nurse, helps writers in the cut-throat world of movie-making. In his blog he lists (happily for a hexagon-hunting six-packer like me) six 'Tips for Vastly Improving your Scripts' in which he distils everything down to action and dialogue, followed by some very short paragraphs which all hinge on the hard work of making things simple, pared-down and super-clear. In other words, in order to be creative, you have to have simplicity.[16] But I think it's the other way round too: in order to be simple and not cluttered, you often have to be creative.

Here's an example from business. Henry is a British entrepreneur who founded Nonsuch, the drinks company which brews a new kind of delicious non-alcoholic mixer called Shrub. This market is likely to be worth over $2 *billion* by the mid-2020s, and to mix my metaphors, Henry would like a large slice of that pie. He stands a good chance of doing so because he belongs to one of the oldest family drinks businesses in Britain. Back in 1728 Clement Chevallier, Henry's five times great-grandfather, planted a cider orchard on his land in Suffolk. This orchard grew into a multimillion pound business producing famous apple juice, cider and cider vinegar. I have been drinking anything Henry makes ever since because he is a culinary and commercial genius. Just like the chefs he knows who are already recognized for their culinary creativity, Henry brought an artisan approach to flavour, colour and brand into a highly competitive market. Yet if you asked Henry whether he is creative he might scratch his head, look slightly puzzled and say he wasn't. Yet the successful branding and marketing of his business relies intensely on both creativity and simplicity in harmony together: customers have to connect quickly and easily to brands in order for them to 'stick'.

The creative professional

Where else is creativity married with simplicity? You don't expect to find it in the optometrist's chair, amongst all the eye-testing machines, but then you haven't met Layla, 50, a South African-born health professional living in London. Layla trained 30 years ago in the practice of detecting problems in vision as well as early warning signs of other conditions ranging from diabetes to brain tumours. Layla is always bright with colour and usually wears clothes with interesting textures. 'I always refused to wear the white coat' she told me, 'because it's too impersonal, too formal. You can't connect to people unless you really talk to them and any barrier in a diagnostic situation can be a bad barrier.'

This in itself is a creative approach, but there's more. Layla describes how she does her job. Medicine has unlimited different specialisms and Layla's is the condition of low vision, which is essentially a complicated way of needing a combination of glasses, or contact lenses, or medication or eye surgery: her job is to find the simplest solution to her patient's particular issue. There are pretty fixed rules about diagnosis – that's what training is for, medical 'peer review' papers, best practice and so on. But what's interesting is how Layla goes about treating patients after diagnosis. She says:

> There are basic principles with monovision which apply and don't deviate much, and there is only ever a handful of symptoms, so in that sense it's simple. But I have to assess each person individually and I want to keep solutions simple not least because I need to get my patients in and out relatively quickly, but also I believe that unless you provide a simple solution to a person they won't want the solution you give them. In other words, if I give a busy person a pair of contact lenses plus glasses, they may just feel that isn't a solution for them, because it's too busy. On the other hand, I can't literally apply one-size-fits all because there are different available options, some of which are more fiddly than others. I have to listen to them, watch them, and make a judgement before I offer what I think will work well for them.

In other words, white coat or not, this health professional, in order to keep it simple, is being creative – and vice versa.

Layla's and her patients' Individuality, and her creativity, all lead to the simple solution for them – the simplest *available* solution which is *individualized*. It's also good business by the way: if Layla is ever unavailable for an appointment, I cancel and wait until she's free.

The creative robot

So far I have focused on human creativity. Don's script nurse, Henry's non-alcoholic drinks mixers, and Layla's low-vision solutions all come from their identity, their minds and individual types. What about creative technology? I'll confess that I used to be the kind of person who thought that humans were always going to be infinitely superior to machines. Now I know I was being simplistic. What I now know is that humans are always going to be *different* from machines, and that human Individuality and creativity will never be recreated perfectly by artificial intelligence. It will only ever be simulated, or manufactured, the equivalent of something mass-produced versus handmade. But that this reality does not mean something special and unique cannot be created from a *mix* of human and machine, something which can simplify our world for the better.

My poster-child for this is a children-orientated robot called AV1 from a company called No Isolation. Invented in Norway, this robot allows sick children who cannot go to school to both learn and feel connected to their classrooms and classmates. The idea is – of course – simple. A robot gives 'telepresence' – sitting in the classroom, on a desk, in place of the ill and absent child. It can swivel and rotate, and has shown remarkable emotional connection with whoever holds it or connects with it. No Isolation was founded by Karen Dolva when she was in her 20s. Given that in some countries the number of children with chronic illness and unable to participate in education can be edging towards 10 per cent, there is a clear commercial need for No Isolation – and a simple, solution to isolation which puts the Individuality of each child into the presence of a pint-sized robot. I call that creative.[17]

What I especially like about AV1 is that it is a solution for individual children so that they can stay in the group. It is, literally, about ending social isolation. Individuality does not mean alienation and isolation, something we risk forgetting if we spend too much time on social media, which can raise individual voices to a horrible clamour.

I cannot dance like the creative expressionist Twyla Tharp. I cannot draw or paint either. And I'm not an inventor. Does this mean I am not creative? I used to think so. Now I allow myself to think otherwise. Reading people like Twyla Tharp and learning through teaching others about productivity and simplicity has persuaded me that creativity really *is* inside all of us, after all. More than this, when you access it, boom! All sorts of obstacles clear and you can get right on with what you were always meant to do.

All those creative juices work best, however, if mixed well with another quality which can also seem elusive: Integrity.

Integrity

Web of lies

One of the most successful start-ups in the world is a tiny company from Finland called Happy or Not.[18] If you have ever been through an airport security queue you have probably used their product. It is a satisfaction survey machine in the shape of four big simple buttons, ranging from an upturned smiley green to a downturned angry red. It's simple and creative. They now have more than 25,000 terminals in place around the world, not just airports. The simplicity of both the concept (gather passenger feedback for the airport) and design (the buttons are so big you can press them as you pass without actually stopping) is the cornerstone of their success.

But one thing which works so well is that people like to tell the truth. So the Happy or Not clients who want to know whether they are getting it right with their customers – is getting something pretty accurate thanks to this device. Why? Because on balance people are truthful and on balance people have integrity.

The one thing we know about a lack of honesty – or a lie – is that it is complicated. The original phrase, dating back to the Middle Ages, was 'a tissue of lies'. A tissue was a cloth whose weaving was complex and interlaced. Fast-forward to nearly modern times, that is just two centuries ago in 1800, and *The London Journal* published this example:

> The ingenuity and cunning of politicians are not infrequently
> employed to conceal or misinterpret facts; and venal writers are easily
> found, ready to construct a tissue of lies to serve the purposes of their
> employers.

In short: not being truthful is a lot more complicated than being so. Honesty, and integrity (which means 'being honest and having strong moral principles') are the watchwords of simplicity. I'm not just suggesting you have integrity so you will be a moral and good person. I'm saying it is a whole lot simpler if you are.

In society we don't always value integrity. Politics itself has become very compromised by what was called 'truthiness' a phrase started in the mid-2000s. This was the time when the internet exploded the scale and speed at which information and its opposite, misinformation, could circulate. Today we argue endlessly on TV networks and social networks about what is true, or 'fake news' or even 'deep fake'. But it isn't that complicated. We may accept lies, we may even welcome them for entertainment purposes and even if we aren't entirely sure we know one simple thing: the difference between right and wrong.

This is the Simplicity Principle approach to integrity. Keep to facts where you can, like 'take whatever route you want' when driving, but whatever you do, get to your destination in one piece, get to a place that's morally right, not morally wrong. Trust your gut, trust the facts, trust what is being presented to you: *keep it real*. Use tactics, such as 'mirror, signal, manoeuvre' and don't drive head on into something or someone else. Being complicated, following a tissue of lies, will get you into a crash. Tissues of lies unravel. I'm not suggesting you knowingly lie by the way, but many of us *keep quiet* when we know something is wrong. We don't raise our heads above the parapet, because we don't want to get into trouble, or we tell ourselves we don't want to get others into trouble. But often we are afraid to be individual, to speak up and out, and so we draw ourselves into webs of complication.

3Cs: Calling it out, Compassion, Compromise

There is a failsafe to keep you on track with integrity, to keep you on the right side of the simple road and avoiding the web of side roads known as complexity. I call this the 3Cs, and here they are in a nutshell:

- **Calling it out** – no matter how lowly you are in the hierarchy at work, or how shy and introverted, when you know something is not right you must say so. This could be an impossible deadline, or it could be a situation in which someone will come to harm. Calling it out is often especially difficult – and therefore avoided – in workplaces, because of toxic workplace cultures where fear and not collaboration have become the norm. But unless bosses and managers learn to listen to bad news, such as 'I'm sorry but we can't make this work like this', they won't get to whatever workaround is being proposed instead. Calling it out is about being centred in what's real. *Keep it real*, call it out. Much simpler.

- **Compassion** – Oh my goodness, don't we need this one. Compassion, consideration for others, thinking of their perspective is not just about having moral fibre and integrity but something else. You feel so great and so much great stuff happens when you have compassion. It is so easy in these times of anger, times when social media feeds and news feeds are full of hatred and argument, of extreme things happening, to realize that every person deserves a hug, some sympathy. Don't come back at me with 'yes, but what about serial killers?' I get that not everyone deserves an easy ride, but let's focus on us, the majority, the vast, vast, huge majority who may be different, who may feel and think and act in ways which we do not agree with, but who deserve compassion. Research shows pretty clearly that when we act with compassion it is good for us. Take the study conducted over five years by Michael J Poulin at the University of Buffalo which followed 846 people and concluded that those who help others don't just experience higher wellbeing but enjoy a bigger buffer against stress and even longer life itself.[19]

- **Compromise** – Yes. You. Can. Compromise is often something we twist away from, thinking there is only one truth, only one way, and this mindset brings impracticality, complexity, and headaches. Compromise, the making of concessions in order to reach agreement, has to happen: in families, in romantic relationships, in friendships, in work situations and, most of all, with ourselves. If you are the kind of person who thinks you have to be 100 per cent on your game all the time, you are being hard on yourself, and this means you are probably being hard and unyielding on those round you. If you can simplify the situation and agree the one thing (or the two or even three – don't go above six or it classifies as complex!) and focus on that, working backwards from that simple aim, the rest flows much more easily.

There's one far greater example of someone who individually embodied all three Cs and saved 155 lives in the process: the pilot Captain Chesley Sullenberger – 'Sully' – who saved his US Airways Flight 1549 by crash-landing it on the Hudson River in New York in January 2009. From start to finish the drama in the air took six minutes. After he had safely landed, his decision was queried in an official inquiry lasting months by airline officials who did not believe that the only solution was to crash-land, preferring to believe their digital fight simulations which were different from the true-life experience. In this extraordinary six-minute moment, Captain Sully turned from being a pilot trained to follow rules and only rules, into a human with agency over his machine. He became an individual. He called out that the computers must have it wrong, he showed deep compassion for his own life and others by not panicking but keeping cool and calm, and he compromised: he landed on water which was risky and not ideal but the best he could do when the alternative would have been to crash into buildings and sidewalks in midtown Manhattan. He later said this: 'The facts tell us what to do and how to do it, but it is our humanity which tells us that we must do something and why we must do it.'

I feel very moved by these heroic tales and I do know that integrity is alive and well behind the scenes in offices and schools, government buildings and factories the world over. It would be good to know more of them. To have a hashtag #callingitout or #integritywatch which applauds anyone who stands up and says not so much 'No' as 'Let's do it like this instead.'

We're nearly through this chapter on Individuality and there is just one more aspect to cover, and that is where our selves – our blended selves, our individual and group selves – position ourselves: how does the Simplicity Principle apply to Place?

Place

Location, location, location

We tend to think of location as being important in real estate terms, for homes and offices. Everyone knows what a 'prime location' is. But what does this mean in terms of where we place *ourselves*, in our lives? Writing in his gorgeous little book of observation *The Mind of the Bees,* Julien Françon observed that 'their day's work is but a succession of journeys, sometimes distant, always profitable'. A colony of bees, let's recall, really is a group, as large as a small town some 20,000-strong whose occupants are, as Monsieur Françon says, 'by turns architects, masons, scavengers, decorators, quartermasters, chemical experts, tender nurses, and at times savage warriors'.

The bee always goes home – to the hive – or builds a home. The sense of place for bees, both in terms of where they live and also where they go out to, is incredibly strong. And for all the collective unity, each bee has a distinct self, blended within the whole Purpose of the hive. So does every place they put their time, effort and bodies into. It is the same with us. Where we live, where we work, the distance we travel between the two: the simplicity of the journey and the arrangement matters a great deal.

But for the Blended Self, those of us increasingly zigzagging in our lives between different roles, it also involves zigzagging between different locations: literally and figuratively speaking. Locations, not just two, where we place *ourselves* matter a great deal. Why? Well firstly, time. Remember those stubborn hours don't stretch, and by the time you have done with sleeping and generally getting up and about and factored in some general pootling time as I call it (time to water your plants or browse online or shout at the kids) and then got ready for bed again you can't stretch much beyond 15 hours in a day end-to-end. So how we use our time and how much of it we spend travelling is important, obviously. I'll come back to this in the Time section in Chapter 9.

But place, the actual *where* matters, because if it didn't we would never have developed our skills for decoration, for personalizing spaces, for putting our Individuality into wherever we are. In the 1980s the trend in office space was all 'cube farms' – tiny cubicles, jammed in a bit like chickens in a coop. It was there that you could see most clearly the Individuality of a worker: in the desk knick-knacks, the photos of loved ones, the messy desks, the tidy desks. The spaces which say 'this is me'.

Today our Individuality in our places is getting, you guessed it, more complicated. More and more of us are becoming freelance and working partly from home and partly from a variety of offices, co-working spaces, hot desks or cafes.

Pete was a very senior global corporate executive. He looked after the reputation of one of the world's largest communications firms, and spent at least half of every month in the air, shuttling between locations. This is the kind of guy for whom suitcase advertisements on Instagram is designed. He would be keenly interested in the minute differences in weight or capacity, or the new wheels: anything to both ease the boredom of constant travel and stimulate his urge to somehow control a situation which was never in his control. Pete often had less than 24 hours' notice before he had to leave his family and get on a plane. Pete and I used to find time to meet. Sometimes we met abroad: I remember a particularly wonderful evening of cocktails in Mumbai with him, and another in New York. But mostly we met in London, in the Strand, and we would always, always, always, talk about our work–life balance lives, and always, always, always I realized we were talking about travel and place.

Pete convinced himself, as many of us do, that where we live and work 'just is'. That we have no control. Pete is a generous and warm, optimistic kind of a guy and he felt his job and his life were pretty wonderful. He paid no attention to the travel, the split loca-tion. He just accepted it. He did not need to show integrity or call it out or even have compassion for himself, because he felt no conflict. There was just one problem: his body did. Several years into this punishing regime, his body gave out. Rather like worker bees, the ones who do all the heavy lifting, and whose lives are super-short compared with drones and the queen. Worker bees live perhaps 2–3 weeks compared to the queen, who is fed and watered and produces 400,000 eggs in her lifetime but lives for at least 2–3 years. The lazybones drones, who do nothing but wait to be picked to fertilize the queen, are also fed and watered by up to six workers. There was no doubt about it: Pete was a worker bee, steadily sacrificing his life for The Hive or, in modern terms, The Corporation.

One day, Pete's body almost gave out. He developed acute symptoms of a digestive disorder which landed him in hospital followed by emergency surgery. Suddenly, travel was out of the question. As he recovered, Pete found that he did not hanker after the air travel, and instead, began to look afresh at what his individual life required, because, as he told me: 'It's simple, Julia: I'd like to stay alive and watch my kids grow up.' Pete found to his shock that his optimistic acceptance of the status quo had masked a reality. The travel schedule was complex, the working around endless time zones and different teams on different continents, combined with the complexity of being part of a global company at such a senior level was giving him an age-old problem: burnout. As he recovered, Pete discovered that he could make a simple decision: he would continue with his job, but based only in the UK with limited short-haul travel. Instead of thinking this was complicated, he used the Clarity model. He decided. Instead of trying to belong to the corporate Groupthink, he connected with his Individuality and created a workaround which his bosses and colleagues (who valued him hugely) would accept.

These days, Pete and I still meet for cocktails. But we tend to talk about the complex state of the world, rather than the complex state of our lives. Our lives are no less busy, our children are growing, and we talk about them, our spouses, but we talk more about ideas than we do logistics. We talk less like worker bees about to expire from exhaustion as we hunt the nectar, returning laden to the hive, only to toil away again and again. For Pete, place has become a state of mind.

SIX
FIX

INDIVIDUALITY

1   **Be the Snowflake.** Reclaim the idea of being a 'Snowflake' and think of sensitivity/ neurodiversity not as a negative, politically motivated concept but one based on reality, compassion and embracing difference.

2   **Be your true creative self.** Remember that who you are online is not the same person exactly, and that the real you is the one to stay connected with above all others. And notice your creativity even in the ordinary everyday.

3   **Be wary of groupthink.** We all want to belong but to follow what everyone else is doing with blind faith leads to a closed not an open mindset. You can hold a different view to the others, you know.

4   **Be the Chief Happiness Officer.** Ask if you can be the person who inspires and champions wellbeing because you embody it yourself. Use creativity to guide wellbeing.

5   **Have integrity.** Often we are afraid to be individual and to raise our head above the parapet. The result? We draw ourselves into a tangled web of complication. Remember the three 3Cs: Calling it out, Compassion, Compromise. This is about being practical and centred in what is real: it's not so much 'No' as 'Let's do it like this instead'.

6   **Know your place.** The honey bee always goes home or builds a new home. The sense of place for bees, both in terms of where they live and also where they go out to, is incredibly strong. Where we live, where we work, the distance we travel between the two: the simplicity of the journey and the arrangement matters a great deal.

6

Side 3: Reset

The always-on mind needs rest

I look down at my phone and wonder if it isn't its own kind of sensory deprivation chamber. That tiny, glowing world of metrics cannot compare to this one, which speaks to me in breezes, light and shadow, and the unruly, indescribable detail of the real.[1]

JENNY ODELL

Did you know that Saturday got its name because of the planet Saturn which is the sixth planet from the sun? Saturn has, as it happens, its very own hexagon: a hexagonal cloud pattern around its north pole, first discovered in 1981. Saturn is also a Roman god associated with ruling Earth during a time of happiness. This is the kind of fact which has me at 'hello'. As the sixth day of the week, Saturday is commonly the first day of the weekend in most Western countries. That means, really, that six days of the week we are somehow working – even if we are spending a Saturday not working for our jobs, chances are we will be working to organize our life in some way. Always-on is not a good look or feel. We are constantly touching our smartphones (80 times a day), grazing online, sharing socially, being available to our bosses, watching TV in taxis, and being sold apps to download to help us sleep because we are often too anxious, wired and overloaded to know how to power down. Unlike our devices, which at least do have an off-switch, increasingly the question is: do we?

In electronics terms, reset means 'set to zero'. The idea of transposing this 'Reset' concept – a screen wipe – to our own heads from time to time speaks strongly to me. After all, it is often directly because of our over-reliance on electronics that we need to reset in the first place. Because Reset is not quite the same as rest: it is more than rest. Nor is it only to do with sleep, which has become something of the poster-child for the idea of wellbeing, along with mindfulness. I see the value in both sleep and mindfulness, of course. Sleep in particular we know as much for what happens if we are deprived of it (nothing good) as we do the benefits of having enough. But rather than dwell on them here or add to an already rich literature on both topics, I want instead to take you in this section on a bit of a journey into what Reset means and feels like, as an experience.

This chapter is really devoted to the idea of Saturn Saturday: that there needs to be a day (or at least a regular way) in which you build up a habit based not on action and doing and engaging but the opposite: powering *down*. Resetting is harder than we might think when our culture values not stopping, not slowing, and reaching much more than zero all the time. Everything is set in society today to build up: build up your followers, acquire more belongings, show how busy (and therefore apparently important) you are with a never-ending to-do list. The idea of going back to start again is somehow regarded as threatening rather than being seen as refreshing.

Let's see if we can look at it through a new lens. Here are the six aspects of Reset as I see it, although, like all the aspects of these axioms, they are just ingredients. You might decide to swap out one for another:

1 **Release:** the off-switch stops always-on
2 **Mind-less-ness:** letting space happen without losing out
3 **Curiosity:** becoming a tourist in your own life
4 **Nature:** being outside as much as inside
5 **Breath:** from the breath to the breather
6 **Fun:** when distraction helps your Social Health

Release

I'm not a junkie or something, I said defensively. I'm taking some time off. This is my year of rest and relaxation.[2]

OTTESSA MOSHFEGH

Stop the world and let me off

'I'm tired of going round and round,' country music legend Merle Haggard wrote in his song *Stop the World and Let Me Off.* He was, of course, writing about love, but I think of how tiring and wretched it is to be shackled to constant connectivity. Electronic, connected life is like love. We need and are hopelessly bound to it, whether we like it or not. The very way algorithms are designed is to trigger our social self-worth and to crave more computer connection, not less. There really isn't such a thing as off-grid any more. It is very, very hard not to need connection of some kind or another in purely practical terms, which is why digital detox is a one-off, rare thing: no one can be un-digital any more. We're all on the digital dancefloor, unable to control our feet as the ground revolves constantly underneath us. Of course we can stop notifications (permanent pinging really should be outlawed) and other hacks to impose limits and curb temptation, but that requires us to be vigilant all the time which in itself is exhausting.

Plus, this is the age of so-called 'hustle culture' in which an increasingly freelance, gig economy workforce is on the rise. *Forbes* reported that half of the workers in the United States will be freelance by 2027.[3] Even if you remain in a single, secure job for a period of time the chances are you will be facing constant retraining and reskilling. According to the World Economic Forum one in four workers has not got the right skills they need in the Age of Automation.[4]

With this kind of daily complexity, it's no wonder we all crave release. Right now, we seem addicted to the wrong kind: alcohol and drugs. The opioid epidemic in the United States and elsewhere has thrown a spotlight on so-called 'legal highs' but it all amounts to the same thing: stop the world and let me off. One of the most poignant novels I have read recently is *My Year of Rest and Relaxation* by Ottessa Moshfegh, which is a terribly stark portrait of desperation, turmoil, hopelessness, and a desire to escape reality fuelled by opioid oblivion. Of course this is fiction, and of course the character has more to contend with in her head than hustling for work. But this novel's literary success is testament to how it speaks to our times: we are literally going out of our minds with exhaustion and dying, also literally, for release.

Small wonder. The more we embrace complexity, the more we turn away from simple solutions and simplicity itself, the worse things get. Release of the wrong kind – oblivion – has become frighteningly normal. The question we should all ask ourselves, before we get to the *how* we achieve release, is *what* are we seeking release from, and especially *why*. The chances are that you will be feeling life is too complex, too overwhelming, too difficult to fix. Remember that Hexagon Action is a route to simplicity: it can help you design something as vital as release in a way which is positive rather than negative. How? Acceptance.

Acceptance

I think if you asked anyone who has an addictive personality of any kind, they will say that the inner critic is a very loud voice.

Given that we are all somewhat addicted to achieve more, faster, further, than ever before, many of us are to some degree experiencing high anxiety. Let's not forget our old enemy stress, which stalks the corridors of power just as it does the confines of our own humble homes. So it stands to reason that release of any kind will only come if you accept that you want and need it. If you give yourself – and indeed others around you – permission. The British writer Johann Hari has probably done more than most to bring out into the open the question of depression and to challenge our use of medication. He puts it simply and very well when he writes that the opposite of addiction isn't sobriety. It's connection.[5] When we accept that we are not happy or fulfilled or that we have deep pain, we accept something about ourselves. That we are social. That, like the bees, we have to belong or else we cannot survive. For me the whole idea of release is that when we accept what we truly feel, this is liberating and a release in itself.

I'm pleased to see that the work culture is definitely moving in the right direction. Wellbeing is rising up the corporate agenda, and when you have a far wider global conversation about mental health than at any time in history, it is a positive sign. But responsibility for what happens in our own heads and hearts is, ultimately, down to us. We have to feel confident that we can establish boundaries to cut and limit stress, and that release can be something we do proactively, to ward off stress, rather than the desperate act to short-circuit it instead.

Standing still

Louise Chester is one of the most trusted advisers to corporate leaders in the world, a former star investment manager in banking, responsible for often lightning-speed investment decisions on many millions of dollars. Her global practice Mindfulness at Work focuses on how being in the present moment is a critical business skill. Louise's Purpose – to enable leaders and whole organizations to make better decisions and be more prosocial and sustainable – has been as impactful on the bottom line as her previous work in investment management. I love Louise for many reasons, not least is that she is always completely honest about her own struggles and challenges, but also because she is a changemaker. I love asking Louise to be my sounding board, in between gossip, walking, cocktails and all the fun stuff we do together. Her take on the Simplicity Principle is really interesting:

> For me simplicity is all about stillness, and releasing yourself from all the reactivity we constantly push ourselves to undertake. It is the quantum space of potential in the middle of the hexagon. The space between stimulus and response that you pivot from.

I realize that she is absolutely right. You can't always release yourself from turmoil or turbulence by moving around and being active. Often, you have do the exact opposite: get to a point of stillness.

For those of us who are already revved up, antsy and anxious, this can seem like a talk ask. But if we let ourselves reconnect to human scale and human *limits* in order to get some release from the pressure of constant complexity, how wonderful would that be? The interesting point about really giving yourself permission to let go, to be still, is that it doesn't actually feel as dramatic or difficult as you imagine it will be.

In addition to letting go in your head, there is also the release from obligation to actual doing. This tracks back of course to an earlier side of simplicity: Clarity, and the question of both Decision and Boundaries. Arianna Huffington puts it beautifully in her groundbreaking book *Thrive* when she talks about release from too many tasks. It was very liberating to realize that I could complete a project simply by dropping it – by eliminating it from my to-do list. Why carry around this unnecessary baggage?[6]

Quite. The second aspect of Reset picks up the theme of letting go. Although you might think I have written it wrong, I haven't.

Instead of focusing on mindfulness, I'd like you to consider the opposite: Mind-less-ness!

Mind-less-ness

Downtime

I once ran a retreat for a group of writers, thinkers and corporate types, and one year we went to the seaside, to the beautiful windy grey English shore of Aldeburgh in Suffolk. One of the speakers was the brilliant Anthony Seldon who offered to take a bunch of people walking before breakfast. Many agreed because having him there was regarded as such a catch. This is a man for whom the word multitasking is an understatement: he was running a major school at the time, in between writing political biographies, and I counted myself lucky that he had agreed to join us.

What our star guests walking group didn't quite know was that this wasn't just a walk and it certainly wasn't a walk-and-talk. This was a mindfulness walk. This was back in the day well before mindfulness was big. The idea of holistic self-help and reflection, the kind which Louise Chester and others have taken mainstream, was some years off. Back then, people thought downtime really meant deprivation, not enrichment. It took someone with my guest speaker's stature in public life to begin to break through layers of ordinary British up-tightness and even suggest such a thing.

Everyone came back wowed and energized both by the sea air and the contemplation. But one guest made a barbed remark: I wish he had advocated mind-*less*-ness instead, he complained. Too much inner reflection, well, *come on*. Even though I knew he was being defensive in his cynicism (and worse, snobbish), I realized he had unwittingly made rather a good point.

Because in order to practise meditation or mindfulness seriously you have to do something, even if it is to set aside time, sit down or walk, or turn on an app. In some ironic way you are turning your mind *on* in order to let it relax and switch *off*. You have to engage with it. And it got me thinking. Why do we tend to assume that mindfulness and meditation are the only ways to achieve serenity and switch off? What if we should be aiming just as seriously for Mind-less-ness – and if so, what is it?

Space to think

I think that the heart of it is space, combined with Louise Chester's sense of stillness. What you call it is, in the end, your own business. It's how you do it that matters. And how you feel. When you stop, even momentarily, and let space into your mind without directing it to think or do anything in particular, it's a form of repair. Making space is a really good corrective for overstretched minds.

The meditation expert Michael Taft once undertook a 92-day silent retreat and commented that he calls the result 'my mind not being full'.[7] Maybe I am splitting hairs here, and making an unnecessary distinction. Well, yes I am. The language we use to motivate ourselves is super important. Some people just body-swerve away from the idea of Mindfulness, like my barbed commentator on the retreat, but does that really matter if he finds another way to reset his mind? No it doesn't. You could say that mindfulness or mind-less-ness are not so different, but how you perceive them is.

Anthony Seldon is one of the most *mindful* people I know, yet he really practises, just like Michael Taft, an emptying of mind. And with good reason. The fact is that the more we discover about the way the human brain works, the more we realize that it works just as hard at resetting and resting as it does performing specific tasks. In neuroscience the Default Mode Network is a relatively recently discovered network part of the brain, representing the meeting point for a number of key pathways which conduct unconscious thinking and processing: the cultural writer about humans and nature Michael Pollan describes this as the place your mind goes when it's wondering or worrying.[8, 9] I wonder whether I will be forgiven for creating a new word: *mindful-less-ness*? It's a pick-and-mix but the truth is, don't we need to do that anyway, when we seek a Reset?

The simple switch-off

Of course, simplicity plays its part regardless of what we call our downtime. Because by weeding out all the limitless possibilities and narrowing our focus, we can begin to achieve a Reset state. When I listen to a piece of classical music or chop a single piece of garlic as part of some cooking preparation, I am simplifying my actions. In slowing my thought processes, I am reaching that increasingly elusive state in our frantic world: Relaxation. I don't value-judge what the switch-off activity is. For many a little bit of online shopping or gaming has the same effect. There is something here about being in privacy too. Switching off can feel private, perhaps because it gives permission to be intimate with ourselves. Out of uniform, out of the character that to some degree we often play out there in our lives. I often find that the signal I send myself to relax and switch off is to be in pyjamas. I don't mean PJs as a fashion statement, wearing expensive casual luxe or anything. I mean actual un-glamorous, privacy-of-my-own-home dressing right down. Not being on, in order to be fully switched off.

This Mum Runs

I have already mentioned the spooky way in which six features a lot in sport: tennis has six games a set; volleyball has six players per team, and a women's basketball is size 6; and in cricket there are six balls in an over. But even if you are not bringing this aspect of

Hexagon Action into play when it comes to Reset, sport is clearly one very good way to achieve switch-off.

The British social enterprise #thismumruns is described by its founder as a happy accident. Mel Bound put a message out on Facebook because she wanted a buddy to run with and to help her get back in shape with two young children and a busy life and commute. TMR as it is known has become a community for thousands of working women with children, all of whom post pictures of themselves looking gloriously reset from the stresses and strains of everyday life. The strapline of their social runs is 'your time, your space, your pace'. Although I'm not a runner, I have become much more involved in sport as I have reached my middle years and understand that there is not much more of a quick fix for 60 minutes than doing something intensely physical like sport. To my surprise I have become passionate about spin cycle classes and am not sure I would have completed this book on schedule without the focus and energy the classes at Psycle in London and Soul Cycle in New York gave me. Group exercise is a really effective switch-off, when you lose your own inner isolation and belong somewhere else in a very different headspace. Even the change of clothes helps, like the PJs. And I confess, yes, not being able to using my phone for a whole 45 minutes can feel like a real achievement!

Curiosity

Curiosity is, in great and generous minds, the first passion and the last.

SAMUEL JOHNSON

Active rest

Of course the idea of Reset is connected to actual resting, and most people's idea of rest is passive, often prone, from lying around on a sofa to lying down with a sleep mask. Andrew Davidson put it very well when he said that his ideal Reset comes from active rest. Andrew and his partner David are big travellers and especially big walkers, both in cities and the countryside. They live in a tiny walk-up apartment in London and in homage to their love of the outdoors have laid a tiny strip of synthetic grass on their minute balcony. If you follow @andymakethetea on Instagram you will see that he is often posting images from his travels. Museums, buildings, light. England, Wales, Scotland and Ireland, the British Isles, all get visited. But so too Europe, America. South Africa. Everywhere interests Andrew because Andrew is endlessly curious about the world and people. This has two effects. First, it makes Andrew a great person to be around. He has huge energy and empathy. This may be partly because he takes a lot of holidays! He definitely knows how to switch off (good for him). But it also makes him wise, because he has seen a lot from wide perspectives. Because when he travels, Andrew looks around. He notices.

Noticing

The social psychologist Adam Galinksy has studied the effects of travel on creativity and concludes that our brains' ability to change through neuroplasticity means that when we immerse ourselves in other cultures through travel our mental health is improved through the opening of new experiences and ideas. Many modern studies show that travel does indeed improve the mind.[10] My father was a writer who was also a great traveller. During his lifetime he loved nothing more than visiting new places and thanks to a successful career he went to many countries. Even in his nineties he went travelling, with my mother organizing a motley crew of medics for emergencies wherever they landed. My happiest childhood memories are of travelling with him to Paris, to New York, and to mountains in North Wales. Now that I do quite a lot of travel I miss him the most when I am about to go somewhere. Often, as I head to the airport, I tell him where I'm going and imagine our conversation. A lump comes to my throat. He is missing this great world!

Dad would almost certainly be able to tell me something about wherever in the world I am going: he had an almost encyclopaedic knowledge as he read anything and everything. After he died, I was sorting through papers and found a bundle of diaries he wrote back in the 1930s. His native language was German but by the time he was a teenager he was living in London and he started to write in English. I was very struck by one account he gave in which he recorded some observations of daily life around him and then wrote to the effect that 'I'm going to start noticing everything. That's what I'm in the business of. Noticing.' In other words, my father, even at an early age, had Curiosity. Curiosity leads people like my father and Andrew to be open, to travel, to reset and regenerate. I think of them as perpetual tourists – of ideas, places, people. For them Curiosity fuels ideas, inspiration, energy. It is more like play than it is like work. Even though it involves a lot of thought and action, it's restful. My dad, like Andrew, worked really hard and then knew how to stop. He used his Curiosity to gain perspective. In the stopping and doing something different, and in fact in noticing others, actively, he was still resting his mind and his senses. He was able to return to whatever he was working on with renewed focus.

Nature

From November to February, the bees rest. It is for us to let them rest, free from irritations and disturbances.[11]

H J WADEY

The hills are alive with the sound of music

When I was a child the movie of the moment was *The Sound of Music*. The image of Julie Andrews, arms outstretched, singing her heart out (and yes, the story is of course about love and loss and danger and rescue), is one of the most memorable in cinema history.

Movies are always a way of taking downtime and time to escape. This movie took very urban audiences – this was the 1960s – out of their heads and into the open air in a way which was literally heady. The countryside was an emblem of freedom, escape and safety. And so it is.

My own family comes originally from the Austrian mountains of Innsbruck, and in childhood we went to almost identical small peaks in North Wales. I grew up with the luck of downtime high up in fresh air, collecting grey slate from the side of moss-covered stones. I drank mountain water so clear and fresh it is still my favourite taste in the world. And I learned that nothing clears your mind more than a good, long, muddy, hard walk – preferably not in pouring rain but ideally with just enough drizzle to make you feel virtuous.

Study after study shows the benefits of being in nature. The University of Berkeley's Greater Good Centre keeps track of findings such as the fact that walking in forests reduces stress and promotes relaxation, evidenced by lower heart rates and higher heart rate variability, and Finnish research that 20 minutes walking in nature reduces stress more than 20 minutes walking in a city does.[12] What strikes me about this is that nature teaches us a little bit of humility: you can't keep up superior airs and graces, job titles or look-at-me-Instagrams when you are amongst all creatures great and small because, well, you realize how silly it all is. Perhaps this is why when you do take stressed-out city people to the countryside and walk around, talking, noticing, connecting with trees and land, something strange happens: people drop pretence, and generally start to relax.

All creatures great and small

Of course, when you walk in nature you come across animals and insects. These words are being written in the middle of the Welsh hills where I have a field of cows rising on one side of the kitchen window, and small group of geese and sheep lurking about nearby. In his book *The Body* Bill Bryson makes the point that for all its powers, nothing about your brain is distinctly human. We use exactly the same components – neurons, axons, ganglia and so on – as a dog or hamster.

Although I am smitten by our two cats, Mitzi and Levi, and by our daughter's dog, a little Jack Russell terrier called Dapple, I have never been an animal lover as such. I am, to this day, a bit scared of cows and horses; I eat meat and would always say if asked to donate either to an animal protection cause or a human protection cause which one I would choose. And yet, once I started to read about bees and become inspired by them, and to spend more time in nature thinking about this book and writing it, it altered my perception of creatures overall. Because as soon as you start to connect both to the rhythm and pace of nature and to notice its creatures, you feel the contrast when you re-emerge: that's the rest, that's the Reset. To go, to disconnect from one kind of being, to connect to another, and then to return: wonderful.

In their book *Not Doing*, Diana Renner and Steven d'Souza describe the connection between nature and humans, animals and rest.[13] One particular scene from Australia stayed with me, describing a woman arriving by a creek in a restless state, learning to tune in to the environment and the horses there:

> She noticed the wild flowers, the flow of the creek, the sway of the branches, the hesitance of the horses, the shivering of the mane. One by one, they walked towards her, standing close. They stood there, not grazing, just standing in relaxed stillness.

The great outdoors

All of this chapter is especially relevant to what I call Social Health, which is how we take out wellbeing into account when we are in a constant state of connection via digital devices, and being 'always on'. While this means, of course, the balance we achieve between being online and offline, it is also to do with how we connect to ourselves and others. It also means whether we live our lives mainly in cities, in a fast and frenzies environment, or whether we achieve space and pace outdoors too. Remember that the Simplicity Principle hinges on balance. Nature is the great re-balancer. Researchers in the Netherlands found that even just looking at a picture of nature's scenery is enough to calm what is called the parasympathetic nervous system.

While I was writing this book, I found myself at my most productive when I was in or close to nature. Although I live in the middle of London, one of the busiest cities in the world, it has some beautiful green spaces and my favourite is one I grew up on the edges of, Hampstead Heath. A huge and ancient area of woodland in the middle of what is now north London, it is one of the capital's great attractions for tourists and Londoners alike. Hidden in the middle, down a little track surrounded by trees is the Ladies' Pond, a tiny oasis where women much braver than I swim year-round. But in the summer and early autumn I take cold-water swims to clear my head and focus my mind. Being surrounded by nothing but the gentle chatter of other bathers and sharing the bracing water with a bunch of ducks and nothing but clear sky is simply beautiful. I found myself making my own routines simpler, less cluttered. I wanted to live the values I am recommending to you. As I did so, I began to change. I noticed it in small ways. I became tidier. Neater. I stopped being quite so busy quite so much of the time, because I did less. I took time to notice what I was doing in a calmer way. I'm not as brave as Sophie Levey who swims year-round in the North Sea near her home on the coast (and who has been known to march me into Welsh cold-water rivers and giggle as I yelp in protest) – but being on Hampstead Heath a lot? That I can handle.

At a time when we are realizing the dangers an overly complex world is in in terms of the climate, and all the ways in which we live and consume, a simpler system and simpler life beckons.

Breath

Once, on a plane, I experienced a full-blown panic attack in heavy turbulence. I can remember hearing someone (it turned out to be me) moaning loudly and I can recall feeling utterly disconnected from my body. The next thing I knew, a wonderful flight attendant threw all my bags off the seat next to me, sat down, handed me a brown paper bag, and calmly told me to breathe steadily into it. My panic and my breathing slowed instantly, just as the plane itself stopped jerking uncontrollably and resumed its calm way through the night sky.

How we breathe, and indeed how often, is pretty remarkable. In his wonderful book *The Body* Bill Bryson explains that:

> Quietly and rhythmically, awake or asleep, generally without thought, every day you breathe in and out about twenty thousand times…
> 7.3 million breaths between birthdays, 550 million or so over the course of a lifetime.

Honey bees, my poster-species for Simplicity and Social Health and indeed Hexagon Action, don't actually breathe as such, although they need oxygen just as much as we do. They use a network of spaces called spiracles with which to suck oxygen directly into their bodies. Let's not forget that one of the key reasons why bees make their hives out of hexagons is because its space efficiency allows the oxygen to flow well through it without wasting energy. But even if they don't hyperventilate like we do when stressed, bees do actually get stressed and panicked too, especially when foraging doesn't go well. It turns out that bee stress, along with pesticides, is one of the key reasons why bee colonies have been on such a sharp decline.[14]

For humans, breathing well or badly is clearly key to how well we cope, which is not surprising, given that to breathe is to be alive. In no particular order, breathing well improves digestion, the lymphatic system, calms the nervous system, and is a natural pain-killer. After that experience on the plane I realized two things. Firstly, I needed to look at what was making me so anxious (it turned out mainly to be separation anxiety as I began to travel again after some years break when my children were little), but secondly, what was this wonderful thing you could do with breath to achieve a restful, calm state? Even in those two minutes at altitude, I wanted to know more. Could I experience the same calm, without a paper bag and on the ground? Although I was a little late to the party when it comes to understanding just how important a stress-buster a good breathing technique is, I'm now a firm advocate.

The way I do it is super simple. I sit or lie down, I close my eyes, and I breathe in and out through my nose. Sometimes I count up and down to 10 (or 6!) and sometimes I don't. Sometimes I do a little bee-like waggle dance and alter the style of my breath, breathing sharply in for instance and holding it in, but often I just, well, breathe. Every time my attention wanders, I just focus on the breath. Usually I do between 6 and 12 minutes, setting my phone timer.

Without question the easiest, simplest way to untangle the complexities you may be feeling is a bit of breathing. Thanks to the myriad of websites, apps, books and the rise of yoga and mindfulness in the fitness and health world, you won't be short of options – although the best one-stop-shop has to be Thriveglobal. com, set up by Arianna Huffington, and where I'm pleased to contribute as editor-at-large. Even if you are the biggest overthinker on the planet, techniques to calm, quiet, and relax a frantic mind just through breath are worth exploring.

My late brother Joss, whom I only met in my thirties (it's a long story but he was a half-brother), was a theatre director. We talked a lot about feelings, stress, family drama. He always said to me as something of a signature signoff when we parted, either on the phone or with a hug in person, 'keep breathing deeply' and in times of trouble, I always think of him and I always do.

Taking a breather

Learning how to breathe properly to reset and calm oneself is not quite the same as taking a breather. That's a phrase whose origin no one can quite pinpoint, but which everyone understands. 'Let's take a breather' tends to be something of a short-term handbrake applied to a situation. That moment on a humid day when a meeting is not resolving anything. Or when you've been at something for so long, but nothing is really moving.

Taking a breather is a uniquely human thing to do. Again, it's about resting and resetting something, rather than switching off from it completely, as in sleeping. I think of taking a breather as being like that moment you tear yourself away from the screen and just stop. Or step away from an argument. Or just take a break in the middle of something quite intense. It takes a moment to adjust: your adrenaline may still be running on as if you're still there but it doesn't take long at all to readjust. Taking a breather can dramatically alter what happens next. According to an article on emotion in negotiations in the *Harvard Business Review*, in heated negotiations, hitting the pause button can be the smartest play.[15]

There is no reason why the concept of taking a breather can't be extended into situations designed to increase perspective, rather like Mind-less-ness could do. The Simplicity Principle says that you should apply KISS, learn from nature's systems and structure, and behave like a bee. So how about a six-minute breather, or let's regroup outside for a moment and talk through our six essential outstanding issues on this matter, or just let's remind ourselves who needs to do what to get over this hump, or back on board. Overall, I regard taking a breather as a moment to breathe life into something which is flagging, whether that's you, or the focus or enthusiasm for something. It's a way to get a bit of control back, quite naturally.

But the tried and tested breather for me, one which slows my breath and calms and resets me, is the snooze, the nap... the siesta.

Napping

If you asked me for my biggest simplicity hack about rest and Reset, it's the nap. That delicious 20 minutes when you shut your eyes and shut out the world during the daytime. One name for the nap is of course the siesta, whose very name originates from the Latin *hora sexta* which means the sixth hour, ie noon. For me the nap is all about something fast, effective, and simple: the only accessory I insist on is a sleep mask (don't ask me how big my collection is, but you always know what you can buy me for my birthday).

The importance of sleep cannot really be overestimated. Thanks to people like Arianna Huffington, discussing it has become mainstream. The essence of sleep is that the body and mind require us to spend one-third of our lives asleep in order for cells to rejuvenate and repair, and vital hormones to set at the right levels. Humans are what's called monophasic sleepers, meaning we sleep in long single periods and oddly, so do our friends the bees. But most animals are polyphasic sleepers, meaning that, rather like your dog or cat, they nap.

One of the reasons why we need more naps now is because, thanks to digital overload, intrusive stimulation from smartphone, and stress, our sleeping has become much more interrupted: the connection between teenage sleep disorder and new media screen time is especially stark. Mid-life for women is known to bring interrupted sleep thanks to hormonal changes during the menopause, while insomnia or the inability to fall asleep is clearly on the rise, given how big the market in drugs to treat insomnia is becoming. The more complex our lives are, the more complicated our relationship to getting to sleep seems to become. Unpacking the exact elements which might make sleep less elusive or more restful is in itself inexact and exhausting. All of which is why naps, those quick-fix top-ups, come in very handy.

Unlike some of the Reset recipes outlined here, I don't think napping is a good thing to do in a group – save that for swaddled babies in cots, not adults. But there is no reason not to go solo. All sorts of fancy brands have come on to the market to profit from the new corporate wellness, to capitalize on the science that a short siesta can re-energize and refocus an employee in no time. These are basically futuristic-looking designer chairs. I confess I'm not picky about my naps as long as I have somewhere horizontal and often take mine in my car (parked, seat flat, with the engine off!) between meetings.

The truth is, a nap doesn't have to be long or to take place anywhere special. A six-minute nap is not as good as a 16-minute one, but 60 minutes? That's a bit long. Generally speaking, around 20 minutes is a perfect amount of time for revival. I know people call it a power nap, but the only thing powerful about a nap is the decision to have one.

Finally, resetting and rejuvenating doesn't just come from rest, but from the opposite, from action. And specifically, from fun.

Fun

If you never did you should. These things are fun, and fun is good.
DR SEUSS

Momentary escape

Dr Seuss is a good pick-me-up for any adult or child wanting a bit of fun. The wit and wisdom contained in the funny stories of odd creatures doing incredible things – like an elephant sitting on an egg or a cat in a hat causing chaos with kids whose mother is away – are all one way to escape into books. I almost called this section escapism, because when you have fun you are escaping the normal serious, weighty concerns and going off into a new area: escaping into the pleasure of art or cinema for instance. But fun is more than escaping. It's being your Blended Self – who you are but with a lighter touch which leaves you refreshed.

The idea of distraction gets a bad press these days, as we associate it with digital distraction, and as you know I'm certainly against the pings and interruptions and have already written earlier about the proven time-suck that devices can cause. But what about wilful distraction? Escaping into a bit of play or fun is not a bad thing, at all. In fact, many physical and psychological markers change when you laugh and relax: the stress hormone cortisol drops, serotonin levels which regulate mood and sleep improve. I saw a wonderful shared YouTube video about a young fox playing on a trampoline that was embedded in a garden so that it was level with the ground and therefore somewhat disguised. He or she was clearly fascinated and surprised by the unexpected bounce and just kept leaping about endlessly. The young fox could have been interchangeable with a small child doing the same. We know how much animals like to play, from grizzly bears rolling about to our own domestic dogs in the grass. We human animals need enjoyment too. Many academic papers such as one in 2009 by Sarah Pressman and colleagues found clear psychosocial and physical measures associated with physical health and wellbeing.[16] What happens when you have fun is that it's another way of taking a breather, of disconnecting from one mode, entering another, and returning with a change in energy and mood.

Egg and spoon

Here's a bit of fun. The egg-and-spoon race has been around for about 150 years and features regularly in school and local sports and community events. Even the idea of it is funny: a race with an egg balanced on a spoon? That's pretty whacky! I love it as a symbol of the Simplicity Principle because it involves balance and is both tricky but straightforward. It can be done by all ages, all abilities, and it's unlikely you will be able to resist a smile if you either watch it or take part in it yourself.

Play for grown-ups in a work setting is a big industry now, the equivalent of bringing egg-and-spoon races into the boardroom on the basis that it unifies people and engages them, but also gets them into another headspace.

There is mounting research to suggest that productivity can be enhanced by a by-product of fun: Happiness. One example is an interesting piece of British research which invited people to rate their feelings on a scale of 1 to 7, with 6 being very happy, and one of the key mood indicators was to show the group comedy sketches by a famous comedian. In other words: When they have fun, how do they rate their levels of happiness? Guess what: highly.[17]

Having fun in a group doesn't have to be about jokes and side-splitting hilarity of course. It can be about amusing and, yes, distracting ways to feel absorbed *away from* usual meetings and formats: this is the rest and Reset aspect in a professional setting. Twyla Tharp writes in her wonderful book *The Creative Habit* about an exercise she uses called A Dozen Eggs in which you begin to curl up in a tight egg-shaped ball and then unfurl into different egg shapes, a sort of mind–body exercise with echoes of yoga but which allows you to name positions and make new ones up. As Twyla says: 'It couldn't be simpler… delights and lifts my spirit and keeps me coming back to Egg.'

It's not just corporates or communities realizing how important happiness is for productivity, but hard-core economists and policy-makers too. I had the pleasure of hanging out in South Korea with Nobel Laureate Joseph Stiglitz, together with the French economist Jean-Paul Fitoussi and the big champion of policies around happiness, Sir Richard Layard of the London School of Economics when we all spoke at an OECD Wellbeing Forum in 2018. We all had great fun as you do at international conferences, where late-night drinks and daytime corridor gossip oil the wheels of big thinking. These three are at the forefront of moves to harness the importance of wellbeing into government thinking around the world. It's Joe Stiglitz's daring claim that GDP is not the only measurement of economic success but wider wellbeing too that led to the OECD introducing their annual Better Life Index to measure such things formally.[18]

The hexagon of fun

Finally, two hexagon objects I would urge you to have fun with. The first is a football, which is a geometric design of perfection, comprised of a mix of hexagons and pentagons. The original modern football (not the earliest ones made with pigs' bladders) are about 150 years old and were made from 18 stitched panels with six sections containing three strips each: that perfect number six again! Given that over three billion people watched the last World Cup, making it the most-watched live television event of the 21st century, I'm taking it that either you or someone you know likes football.

However, if, like me, you don't, you might like to have fun with another hexagon entirely: the quilt. Hexagon-shaped quilts date back to the 18th century and their early names were Honeycomb quilts or Six-Sided Patchwork. I can't think of anything more soothing, restful, or fun than sitting down with a group of women friends quilting in silks and calicoes and echoing *Godey's Lady's Book* of 1835 which declared: 'Perhaps there is no patchwork that is prettier or more ingenious than the hexagon or six-sided or honeycomb patchwork.'

I have a time-saving variation on a theme of quilt-making: I use colouring-in books for a quick, fun distraction. The strapline on the back of *The New Hexagon Colouring Book* I use reads: 'A bounty of glorious hexagons to colour!' Like Dr Seuss's character in *Green Eggs and Ham* I say this to you: try it, try it, you will see how much fun it can be!

SIX
FIX

RESET

1 **Set to zero.** Sleep is vital but so is a wider sense of Reset. How you recharge when you are awake or during waking hours is in your hands. Identify what works for you in order to set your tension levels back to zero.

2 **Mind-less-ness.** Find your way to achieve serenity, switch off and be still – literally or figuratively. Meditation may be your way but it doesn't have to be what anyone else does. Discover what helps you switch off or what excites and stimulates your creative juices.

3 **Active rest.** Seek out a change in scenery and let your Curiosity fuel ideas, inspiration, energy. Notice what is happening, and be a tourist wherever you are. Return with renewed focus.

4 **Be where the bees and trees are!** Reconnect with the rhythm and pace of nature – the great re-balancer – and notice the contrast when you emerge.

5 **Take a breath and a breather.** Sometimes we need a quick Reset, not to switch off entirely. When things get intense, cultivate techniques to calm yourself by focusing on breath, or take a breather – a moment to individually or collectively readjust.

6 **Find a football.** Find the activity which you can do which is unquestionably fun. If you aren't smiling or laughing in your day, you aren't having enough of it!

7

Side 4: Knowledge

Escaping from infobesity must come first

The four stages of a career:
1. Want emails.
2. Respond to emails.
3. Dread emails.
4. Hide under a desk and set up auto-response that says you are now a cotton farmer in Uzbekistan.[1]

MATT HAIG TWEET

My career began in the analogue age, working with typewriters when computers stood on a desk, not in your hand. Hard to believe if you are my children's generation, a Millennial or a Z (or even an Alpha which is next up) but there was no Instagram, Facebook, WeChat, WeKontatke, Bharat Student, Reddit. There was no internet, no rolling news, no YouTube. We are six centuries past the first big knowledge revolution when Johannes Gutenberg, a German inventor, brought the printing press into the world. Today our world explodes with knowledge.

Torkel Klingberg, Professor of Cognitive Neuroscience at the Karolinska Institutet in Sweden, said in his book *The Overflowing Brain,* that 'attention is the portal through which the information flood reaches the brain' but that our brains lack 'boundless capacity' to both pay attention and process attention.[2] The crisis of 'too' much in physical health terms is called obesity when it comes to food. This is why it's useful to see the current state of information overload as *infobesity*. Just as our bodies get clogged and blocked and slowed by too much complex food in too high a quantity, the same is true of knowledge. When it is full of junk (fake news) or we consume it before we have had a chance to digest its source (the internet) it's easy to pile on pounds of knowledge which doesn't do us any good. And yet, just like food, it is vital. We need it, we should enjoy it. We just need to simplify how we absorb it.

The idea for the Simplicity Principle first came to me when I began to think about infobesity and the crisis of information overload. I realized that the way in which ordinary working life and person life was being disrupted by digital life's scale and speed meant that we needed to behave differently, just like we have learned to do around what we eat and how we exercise. Hence the idea of Social Health: active, practical steps to manage, control and organize what we do online and offline. How we handle knowledge is a very good test of this. Do we sink or do we swim?

Here are the six ways to focus on that huge subject about subjects: Knowledge. Taken separately or together, they should make how we consume it more, well, digestible:

1 **Trust:** how to tell fact from fiction

2 **Wisdom:** the true value lies in experience

3 **Known Unknowns:** how to imagine the future now

4 **Learn:** being the teacher and the student

5 **Curate:** making a 'Knowledge Dashboard' cures infobesity

6 **Remember:** knowing the limits of working memory

Trust

Giant camel spiders

The 'news' during the Iraq war that US soldiers serving in the first Gulf War were facing not just guns but giant camel spiders started circulating on email and quickly became 'known' as fact. In an early example of what is now known as 'deep fake', a photograph of a soldier, taken at an angle which made the spider he was holding seem especially large, was widely shared. As it turns out, this spider is from a group called *Solifugae* and 'even where they are very large, in the Middle East, they could be easily squished under a person's shoe'.[3]

Rumour and gossip is not new, but viral spread through the internet is making what we know, and what we trust about what we know, much harder. Trust is invisible but it has tight bonds. If we don't trust what we know about, for instance, the safety of an aeroplane, it makes us nervous to fly. If we think we know that a person is dangerous, a murderer even, we change our behaviour towards them: Malcolm Gladwell has written brilliantly about this in his book *Talking to Strangers*.[4]

The British journalist Jamie Bartlett, who studies human behaviour in the internet age, produced *The Missing Cryptoqueen*, a podcast series for the BBC about Dr Ruja Ignatova, who persuaded a million people to invest in a bogus pyramid selling scheme called OneCoin.[5] OneCoin said it was a new cryptocurrency founded on Blockchain (the technology underpinning digital currency), but as Jamie and his producer discovered, it was all a sham. The problem was that people put all their trust in believing in it, and encouraged their friends and family to invest too. They insisted that they *knew* that OneCoin was not fake. But in fact all they knew was that they trusted the brand and the marketing: not the same thing at all. The OneCoin story is an example of what the writer Margaret Heffernan calls 'wilful blindness'. People wanted a simplistic solution: an impossibly easy way to make money. Many were poor and believed the glossy hype and veneer of educated respectability. They were not to blame for being conned. However, this story reveals how often human nature is deceived by the shiny promise that something complex is in some way better because it is hard to understand. Don Norman of MIT writes in his book *Living with Complexity* about how in many ways humans love complexity for its own sake and gives as an example the odd rules of many sports, or the rituals around how we brew coffee and tea. He's right.[6] But when you exploit this natural curiosity for the complex and use it to defraud, the consequences can be dramatic.

Go back to the last axiom on Reset, and the idea of *noticing*. Start to notice if you can trace the source of knowledge properly, and whether you trust that source. Are you believing what you read or see because you have no reasonable doubt or could the evidence be manufactured? Jamie Bartlett found that the charismatic and expensively dressed Ruja Ignatova appeared to feature on the cover of *Forbes* magazine – a fact which was heavily used in marketing. But on closer inspection, it was a paid-for advertisement in Bulgaria, which was then manipulated into an image with the *Forbes* strapline to look like it was an editorial front cover. On the internet, anything can spread so fast that fiction can become accepted as fact. In fact there is a huge difference between editorial coverage, subject to the strict 5Ws of journalism – the *who, what, why, where* and *when* – and advertising. *The Missing Cryptoqueen* exposed how many global brands were also deceived, in their case *accepting* money from OneCoin in order to unwittingly be used to validate its fraudulent brand. The psychologist Robert Cialdini calls this 'social proof': you trust what others trust and so you perpetuate behaviour.[7]

When it comes to information, especially when someone is trying to get you to act based on information you need to trust, try and keep it simple. Why am I trusting this information – is it a person, a brand, or information I fully understand? Does my gut tell me that this is too complicated for me to understand and that I am being asked to trust someone, a person, rather than facts? Is there a red flag warning I can't put my finger on? All too often we can feel carried along in the rush to fall into line with others, even if this means believing absolute rubbish!

Sometimes trust works the other way: you trust something because it does work, you can prove it works, and, ideally, because you can see it with your own eyes.

Putting a stirrup on a horse

If you need to rethink what you know about camel spiders, what about horses? In their book *Alive: Digital humans and their organizations* Paul Ashcroft and Garrick Jones note that 'a stirrup on a horse is technology that gave Mongols a strategic advantage', referring to the idea that when the pairing of a little foothold with a saddle and a strap was first discovered or created in China in antiquity, the whole of civilization accelerated.[8] Communication, transport and warfare all benefitted from man's ability to control an animal like a horse or mule that much better. Now maybe you know all about how vital horses have been to human history, and maybe you even know that the stirrup changed the course of history.[9] What I want to know is how did horse riders back in the mists of time get to figure out that accessorizing horses made them work better? Well, human ingenuity and probably a lot of trial and error. And trust. Someone had to get on that first stirrup and give it a go.

I want you to be able to tell the difference between knowledge which is useful (a stirrup), the kind which is false but entertaining (soldiers being threatened by camel spiders in the desert) and something else: knowledge given to you which may or may not be true, but you trust because of the way it is expressed – as an opinion.

In my humble opinion

The great journalist and commentator Walter Lippmann once wrote that 'There can be no liberty for a community which lacks the means by which to detect lies.'[10] Although journalism itself admits, famously, that it is only the 'first rough draft of history', a solid media outlet with a trustworthy reputation is going to check its facts far more readily than a random tweet or poorly regulated advertisement on Facebook. That must surely be true, yet what happens when you think you are telling the truth but may in fact be mistaken and therefore misleading others?

Take this book. Both I and my editor Chris Cudmore have worked very hard to get you to trust the information you are reading. It's called fact-checking. Even when I think I'm certain of my facts, I check them, because memory is unreliable: you may know about the psychological experiment which followed the 9/11 terrorist attack. Several hundred people experienced 'false memory' syndrome, mis-recalling where they were, with dramatic differences in their accounts one year on. Even when we are passionate and sincere in our belief of what is true, it may not be.

But I am not just giving checkable facts in here. I'm also giving opinion, which can't be checked, or regulated much. You have to, yes, trust me that I am both sincere and that the context I'm dressing up my facts in makes sense. In this respect I am less an author, as in 'authority', and more of a commentator.

In newspapers and news media the superstars are the commentators and columnists, who command far higher salaries and profiles than the 'backbenchers' because they serve up finely tuned words and views which are in many ways more attractive than the news itself. This is one more layer of complexity around information and knowledge. When you apply the Simplicity Principle you recognize the need to balance on the beam of what is *complicated* and can to some degree be unpicked, and what is *complex*, the much more embedded and hard-to-untangle bits.

So you may say start to unwind the context of this view a bit to get to a simpler version of what you are seeing or hearing: the agenda of the person giving the view, or their media. In other words, ask the simple question: What's the reason for this opinion? Why now? What not another view? This will help you cut through the way in which opinion often forgets a crucial thing: you have a choice about how you interpret it, or whether you believe it at all. Let's go back to the facts. I feel that those five journalism Ws – the who, what, why, where, when – are, of course, missing a perfect sixth: wisdom.

Wisdom

Knowledge workers

According to research, one-sixth of us fit the description 'knowledge worker'.[11] A large amount of what we use is what becomes known as 'institutional knowledge' which is why the headache for HR departments is when someone leaves with information in their head they can't easily or quickly replace: in other words, wisdom. Our beautiful friends the honey bees rely on wisdom when they forage for flowers and pollen. They scout out the best places, and, as a 'social species' use their antennae to communicate the information to their colony, including how to extract the pollen, fly it back to base etc. One of my favourite bee books is *The Lore of the Honeybee*, written back in 1919 by a man with the wonderful name Tickner Edwardes, a clergyman in south-east England, whose big passion was bees. He notes: 'An hereditary, communal intellect evolved through the ages, the sum and total of all bee experience since the world of bees began.'

For humans, dictionary definitions of wisdom include this: 'the quality of having experience, knowledge, and good judgement; the quality of being wise.' Wisdom is more than knowledge. It's a whole bundle of senses which together make us wise. This is perhaps the single reason why humans retain a superiority over machines: no matter how advanced AI is becoming (and it is becoming *very* advanced) it still lags behind us in terms of how we use feelings and judgement, combined with real-world experience. We call inner, instinctive wisdom 'sixth sense', but even what you might call outer wisdom, based on trackable knowledge, isn't easy to pin down.

Wisdom isn't bought like gas at a petrol pump, by volume or weight. It is built up and layered. In this sense, wisdom is soft knowledge. Its edges are blurry and yet it is invaluable. Government security services which call themselves 'intelligence' services are in the market for lots of this soft, wise knowledge: what people understand but can't prove is still what they *know*. Indeed, anti-terror campaigns often encourage the public to trust their instincts, and their inner wisdom that 'something doesn't feel right'.

This goes to the heart of the Simplicity Principle. Even if you can't put it into words, what do you know, what do you feel, what do you sense? What have you experienced? Be the bee in this: use your antennae. Use your sixth sense. Bring this to the table, either the boardroom table or the coffee counter or the meeting room. Bring what you *know already*. I often notice that younger people or people from a less advantaged background don't realize how much wisdom they have. Perhaps because I did not go to university myself but built up what I know through a combination of learning on the job (lots of odd jobs) and self-education (lots of reading, lots of watching, lots of mentors) I know that to be wise comes first from *within*.

Spelling bee

That said, I don't think you can ever know too much or stop learning. I am rather a fan of that wonderful bite-size version of fact, the *factoid*. Much of Twitter seems to be spent (on a good day) sharing this kind of lightweight information with a useful link. It taps into a pretty solid human desire to acquire lots of general knowledge. Most of us have watched a TV quiz show at some point in our lives. *Who Wants to be a Millionaire* has been turned into different language formats in more than two-thirds of the world, in over 160 different languages. It seems that we love watching other people's knowledge being tested, and with it, test our own. The very first TV game show, in pre-internet times, was *Spelling Bee*, and its radio format was called *Information Please*. I grew up with two TV shows which showed off knowledge. *Mastermind* was deliberately intimidating and placed an individual in a chair to be tested on their knowledge with rapid-fire questions from a stern interviewer, and *University Challenge* was a chance for middle-class wise-asses to be pitted against each other. Part of the fun was seeing just how nerdy the contestants were – and how clever. But it is *Millionaire* that kept audiences glued to their screens.

These shows certainly made millionaires of their hosts. In the United States *Family Feud*'s presenter, Steve Harvey, was reported to earn $44 million. What is the real story behind this entertainment? Hard facts, with a simple option: Yes/No or Right/Wrong. Simplicity in a complex world is so sought after that it has endured as a main source of TV entertainment, despite so many other possible formats. We want to know if it is possible, just sometimes, to limit the options and to know what's the answer is. It's worth using this quiz-show technique ourselves: there may often be options, but there are not, when it comes down to it, limitless options, even if we sometimes feel there are. Asking yourself 'what's my final answer?' and pushing for a decision and a choice about what you already know is quite a good – and simple – discipline.

Which brings us to the choppy waters of knowledge which we don't know.

Known Unknowns

Death by PowerPoint

As we know, there are known knowns; there are things we know we know. We also know there are known unknowns; that is to say we know there are some things we do not know.[12]

DONALD RUMSFELD

The minute the words came out of his mouth, I knew they would become legendary. I could not stop thinking about the idea of 'known unknowns' and then I realized why. It was because there was something so serious in the middle of this funny, over-complicated jargon coming out of the mouth of one of the most senior of military figures in the United States. Mr Rumsfeld actually had a point. Sometimes we think we don't know something when in fact we already do. But we overlook them because they are hiding in a thicket of complexity and we stop paying attention. Or, we have such blind faith in our systems that we don't think the unthinkable and ask: 'What *could* happen, even if we hope it won't and even if we don't think it will?' Any combination of these attitudes, often created by complexity, can be deadly. A terrible illustration of this happened a year after Donald Rumsfeld's remarks: the NASA *Columbia* shuttle disaster.

'The *Columbia* is a beautiful ship performing magnificently,' one of the astronauts said happily on camera as the space shuttle was on its apparently normal descent to earth after a routine mission in February 2003. But moments later, something the BBC said 'was so unlikely that no one had ever considered it' happened, and the shuttle broke up, killing that astronaut and six others on board. The unlikely, unknown cause turned out to be a piece of foam coming loose and breaching the spacecraft wing: a true accident. However, there was another explanation. Evidence suggests that these engineering problems were actually war-gamed.[13] Someone had imagined it could happen; they just did not think that it would. So the scenario, Known Unknowns, was presented at NASA several months before the fateful flight. The data was presented in PowerPoint, and in that presentation the attention of those present was dropped or lost.[14,15] I imagine a dimly lit room with people being bombarded with information, not being able to process it fully, and tuning out.

As a result the phrase 'Death by PowerPoint', coined for boring meetings, became all too true. Let's go back a bit to what the cognitive neuroscientist Torkel Klingberg says in his book *The Overflowing Brain:* 'The torrent of information increases not only the volume of data we're expected to take in but also the volume we need to shut out.'

The footage of the mission control room during the last moments of the *Columbia* shuttle is so hard to watch. The flight director doesn't know what we know. He is acting normally. Watchful, in control. He suspects nothing. He believes he knows his shuttle is coming back into land, safely. It is several long moments before he realizes. And in that moment, you see his face. It has a single, stricken tear rolling down his cheek. The camera swings to everyone else and they are frozen in empty horror. Every detail of their body language is searing to see. Because now they know.

While it is true that you only know how risky some outside risk is when it happens – what Nassim Nicholas Taleb calls 'black swan' events because they are so rare[16] – the risk here was known; it was just presented so badly, and with such complexity, that it was not really considered to be a risk, even though it was. Tragically, it was the perfect Known Unknown.

The risk here to the rest of us is clear. You have to imagine and anticipate Known Unknowns if you possibly can. And you have to realize that if you overload people, if you overdose them on information, they may drop their attention just when they need it most. Look into your own situation: can you see the wood for the trees? Would you be alert to the crucial information hiding amongst all the others? If not, can you simplify your systems, processes or the sheer volume of information to make the Known Unknowns come to light?

How to win the Nobel Prize

Sometimes there are very simple experiments and very simple discoveries to be made using what is at hand.

ANDRE GEIM

But now for a good news story. Andre Geim and Konstantin Novoselov won the Nobel Prize in Physics when they discovered graphene, the thinnest and strongest material in the world. When he was interviewed about the work which prompted this tremendous win Andre Geim, a witty and warm man I once met at a private dinner in London, said this:

> For me, it's very boring to deal with the same subject year after year. So, whenever we are doing any particular research, at the same time I'm looking at what else can be done, using the facilities and knowledge we have at hand… Whatever I do, even if I'm working on graphene all the time, I'm thinking, 'OK, what else can the research be used for?' And, usually, it comes out something like late-evening or Friday-night experiments where you try something very elementary and try to go into one or another direction. Ninety-nine times out of a hundred, you do not succeed, but, sometimes there are very simple experiments and very simple discoveries to be made using what is at hand.[17]

What a wonderful example of Hexagon Action! Of applying the 'elementary' to fix something, of embracing simplicity. Of course it is an extra bonus that graphene itself, and carbon, are so tied up with hexagons and sixes: graphene is made from carbon, which, conveniently is number 6 in the periodic table and full of our lucky number six with six protons (and often six neutrons) in their nucleus and another six electrons outside. Over half our bodies are made of carbon. Graphite, a form of carbon, is a crystalline form of carbon and its atoms are formed in hexagonal structures. Out of graphite comes everything from diamonds to solar panels. And out of graphite comes graphene, a one-atom thick layer of carbon which is also arranged in a hexagonal lattice so strong that it is more than 200 times as strong as steel – yet it's the thinnest material known to exist. Since its award-winning discovery graphene has already transformed our knowledge of DNA sequencing, water filters, energy generation and batteries. And sport: the 15-year-old tennis prodigy Cori 'Coco' Gauff uses a tennis racket made of it.

Not fooled by randomness

I wanted to make the point, especially after the grim example of the *Columbia*, that there is plenty of success to be had in anticipating what you don't know, and applying not just simplicity but a sort of surrender to that quest. Nassim Taleb is famous for his 'black swan' theory but he has also written brilliantly about randomness, and how to embrace what you don't know. In his book *Fooled By Randomness* he writes that:

> Probability is not a mere computation of odds on the dice or more complicated variants; it is the acceptance of the lack of certainty in our knowledge and the development of methods for dealing with our ignorance.[18]

This comes back to that Chinese faith in 'flow' (and indeed why the number six is considered lucky in China, because the number six sounds like the word 'flow' in Mandarin meaning everything is going smoothly).

My takeaway on Known Unknowns is really this: to miss something you could and should have predicted is inexcusable. But to *not* know something which you *cannot* know is totally understandable. And different. So don't be afraid to explore what you haven't discovered or thought of yet. Maybe the answer is that you need to know even more, not less. Maybe it's time to become a student, again or for the first time.

Learn

The university of life

I didn't go to university and yet I am a professor. How did that happen? It's a long story, mostly to do with the fact that 'Honorary Visiting Professor' is more of an ideas ambassador than the full time tenured professor: so I run my small business and write and speak more than I teach.

I won't go into my stories of epic early academic failure but certainly at one point my parents were pulling their hair out with worry. I found it hard to concentrate but mainly I found I couldn't connect with anything. I was much more worried about my social group, my clothes, anything but my learning and I found the exam system really off-putting and hard. In our five children I now see that it's completely normal for some to be super good at exams and others to find them as tedious as I did. And how it bears little or no relation at all to ability, talent or future prospects.

I did not go to university and instead did a series of odd jobs in publishing, working my way up and 'learning on the job' as the saying goes. At the time, it was not a standard way to learn. Many of my friends were completing first and sometimes second degrees, which were regarded essential to progress into 'good' jobs. I look back on my early career path, and think I was rather like a small creature burrowing through layers of earth to make my own tunnel. I worked sideways in publishing, television, politics, public relations, and in the end became what I am today: my own employer.

The truth is that there are different schools of thought about whether formal, structured academic learning for a long set period of time in a university setting is as good as learning on the job and acquiring constant new qualifications and experiences. Clearly the answer is that it depends very much on exactly what you are learning and whether it can be combined with a day job or not. We must not make the mistake of thinking that a downloadable PDF is going to have the same learning impact as a good teacher, and yet the rise of MOOCs (massive open online courses) and distance-learning via the internet is also tremendously valid. In the workplace 'digital academies' can provide very valuable ways of flexible learning alongside flexible working. But one thing is worth bearing in mind. The world is moving so fast, and the ladder of opportunity is so limited, that in the end it may make more sense to jump on it and learn as you go, rather than to stay out of the job market while you wait to 'finish' your education. Is education, life and learning ever finished anyway?

Physician, heal thyself

I opened this book with a quote from *The Mind of the Bees* – 'The best bee in the world can teach only what she herself knows' that and I have become a teacher, and enjoy very much sharing and passing on what I have learned. Perhaps because I think of myself first as a student and second as a teacher, when I watch my students who are usually working men and women trying to career-change, I feel that I am practising what I preach. To be a good teacher is to be a good learner. After my father died, my husband spent two years sorting through his library, books, papers and articles so that they could be dispersed to a university archive. My father was an avid reader. He never stopped learning. We now have the shelves fitted in our house and some of the books have found an eager home with our eldest son, a keen student of ideas. I like to think that my father's thirst for knowledge is part of the walls now. When my dad passed away I learned that students in Brazil, where his work was very popular, hung banners outside the dormitories which read '*Viva Hobsbawm!*' What he taught them in his books would live on beyond him. That is the highest praise any teacher or writer can ask for.

The skills gap

In many ways, as a fan of the geometric and the structured, I do wish I had a formal higher education. I do wish I had worked my way methodically through a certain literature to become more knowledgeable. And yet I realize that I can communicate what I know without needing to have anything more than my own curiosity, learning and an audience. The luck of personality and upbringing has given me something which some people have naturally and others can learn: soft skills.

The university of life has a lot to be said for it now that we have to constantly reskill and learn to adapt to artificial intelligence taking some jobs and replacing them with others. The global business consultancy McKinsey reckons that over 80 per cent of big business leaders think retraining and reskilling has to be done for half their workforces in order to address 'the skills gap'.[19] If you plan on working in a very specialist, technical area, or you want to follow the footsteps of Nobel laureate Andre Geim, you need carbon-hard qualifications. The hard skills revolution hasn't gone away, it has just rebooted for the 21st century.

But there are other skills which are now very valuable indeed. These are the soft skills. From eye contact to empathy, from complex problem-solving to team work, reliability and adaptability: these are the skills, in our robotic, automated times, which keep us human, and which we can learn and improve on.

The complex modern world of work, with AI replacing old jobs and new jobs requiring new skills, means that many of the world's top companies, from IBM and Google to EY and Hilton, are ditching requirement for degrees for some entry-level staff, as they value soft skills just as highly. We are not the only species which adapts and learns. The honey bee, our poster-species, has adapted to learn from nature and to be teacher and student at the same time. This is quite unusual in the insect world, except that bees, as we know, are social insects, and they belong to a group which therefore learns, shares, and adapts to knowledge. You could say that honey bees are on a constant quest to reskill. Bees take in everything from the position of the sun and therefore the time of day, to the location and smell of certain flowers. Their teaching consists, rather delightfully, of something called the 'waggle dance', in which they relay to other bees the location of good pollen. In my youth if you studied communication this was regarded as distinctly inferior to the hard sciences. But as the bees are showing, soft skills may be exactly what you need.

The soft skills revolution

How do you get these soft skills? Some of them of course are natural. They come back to the OCEAN personality test in the second side of simplicity: Individuality. Where you are on the spectrum from introvert to extrovert, for instance, or whether you have 'adaptability'. To some degree or another, these skills can be taught. They can be experienced and copied, learned and practised. They are increasingly valued in the workplace.

The very idea of human qualities as a complement to skills has been picked up by a digital skills app from a company called Qdooz, which I advised in the UK when they started up. Qdooz was created by the British corporate mentor, David CM Carter, who wanted to bring confidence and specialist knowledge of coaching and training at scale.

Qdooz point out that not only is it morally right to 'ignite potential' in everyone, but that soft skills can boost lifetime earnings by up to 14 per cent. In a survey of UK executives they found that 92 per cent value soft skills as a critical factor when screening candidates. They produced for the first time a National Qualities Index: 'focused' and 'reliable' were both in the top 10.[20]

Those words matter because what employers want is not complicated. They want productivity. I want it too, both as someone who employs others and who is self-employed. Whatever you are learning or have learned, when it comes to work the question for me is not just what do you know, but what do you do?

M is for motivation

Motivation is a great way to measure Productivity. There is much research, stretching back to the 1950s, to support the idea that employees are more productive when they are motivated, but I like a modern academic study, conducted in Ghana just a few years ago. In this paper researchers[21] studied nearly 500 teaching staff and found that the performance of 80 per cent of them was related to their motivation. The authors cite 'self-motivation by managers' as being the first dimension of motivation. Well, if you are a student or self-employed, you are your own manager. And if you manage others, you know that the simple stuff matters most: whether people know what they are doing, what is expected of them, and that they can deliver reasonably. The minute you have to manage people in a situation which is confusing or excessively complex, the motivation (and concentration) of people drops.

So simplicity strikes again: having motivation propels you towards productivity. If you want to learn, motivation will help you, and if you want to teach it will too. But let's come back to the biggest problem of learning, which is not the method or even the timeframe: it's the Infobesity.

Curate

The Knowledge Dashboard

The 'Knowledge Dashboard' is something I developed to help workshop groups pin down how to think of all their different sources of knowledge. I told them to think of these six sides in a similar way to the 5-a-day health campaigns around a daily intake of 400g of fruit and vegetables. The only reason why a lot of people have in their heads that they ought to eat five portions of fruit and vegetables each day is because it was a very well-run World Health Organization campaign which ran across the world including UK, US, Germany and France. It isn't actually based on five portions, but it stuck because it was so precise.

So the Knowledge Dashboard asks: if you had a healthy intake of knowledge each day, or in any given period, across your organization or just in your own life on your own time, what would that look like? Of course you remember the 6Ws of Knowledge from earlier in this chapter, the who, what, why, where, when of journalism plus my added sixth: *Wisdom*. Apply the same with your Knowledge Dashboard. When you identify six types of information you need to get to grips with it helps you structure, shape and control the flow of information. One of the surest-fire ways to avoid accidentally snacking and building up a state of infobesity.

What exactly do I mean by 'infobesity'? Well, think of ordinary obesity, the kind that the World Health Organization says has tripled since 1975, and which is as bad for global health as it is preventable.[22] Obesity comes from eating too much food which has the wrong kind of nutrients, additives, and which combine lethally with insufficient exercise. Remember that I talk about Social Health, the state of connection in a digital age. Is that healthy? Not if too much information gushes into us, overwhelming us, full of less-than-nutritious and untrustworthy snippets, factoids and all the things which came up earlier in this chapter.

Just like our intake of food and our uptake of exercise to avoid or reduce obesity, there are things we can do to manage the risks of infobesity, and in a word, it's Curation. Curation is to infobesity what portion control is to physical obesity. Curation cuts down and cuts through the fatty tissue of TMI: too much information. And a Knowledge Dashboard is like a carb- or a calorie-counting app: it helps you keep on track.

They key to the Knowledge Dashboard is variety of knowledge groups, just like food groups. You should aim for mix of topics – say three which cover news and views, whatever your specialism is – and then some general entertainment or what I call simply 'Zeitgeist'. And then a mix of mediums: because a tweet or a blog is like a snack compared to the meal of a long read, and listening to a podcast or watching a TED Talk is not quite the same as reading a full-length book. The type of knowledge matters in form and in content. So let's take just a little look at the river of information itself and how Curation can ever get started. It's really all in the Simplicity Principle: Keep It Simple, Sweetie, and *less is more*.

Kill your darlings

Ask yourself how you came to read this book. Either someone recommended it, or a bookseller bought it and put it on their shelves. Or you saw it thanks to the kind of algorithm-based recommendation which says, 'frequently bought together'. Either way, it is a form of Curation, of simplifying an enormous range of possibilities, to a few. In the case of art, or newspapers, or the contents of this book even, Curation is constantly at work: selecting what to put in and what to leave out.

I've already killed many thousands of darlings, as the great writer William Faulkner put it, in order to bring you (hopefully) just the right words. On a daily basis I know that many Curators are at work to bring me the things I read at speed which are curated: Tortoise Media, Brainpickings by Maria Popova, Thrive Global, Flipboard are all examples for me, but so are mainstream media websites and apps. When I open a fashion magazine or app I'm counting on someone curating 'the look' for me and where to buy it.

Having others curate for you is great. But what about when you have to filter information and know what matters for yourself? How do you get to create your Knowledge Dashboard? Knowing what to put in requires you first to think about the opposite: what to leave out. I think that before you can learn what to pay attention to, or ask others to focus on with you, you have to kill some darlings. Look at it from the perspective of office politics. You may have 15 minutes with your boss. You may be absolutely longing to get a whole bunch of stuff off your chest but you can't: you only have that 15 minutes. What do you keep in and what do you discard?

Let's remember what happened to the PowerPoint presentation at NASA which contained vital information which did in fact predict the 'unthinkable' thing which ended up happening: a piece of foam puncturing the carbon tank of the *Columbia* on its descent to earth at incredible speed. I have seen the actual PowerPoint slides on which this information was included and it's a visual mess. It's busy. It's cluttered. It looks complicated. When we look at our basic human cognitive limits, what our brains can handle, we can see that it wasn't that the unthinkable was dismissed as a low risk: it was probably barely even noticed. Way too many darling bits of data went on those slides, and it was way too much to handle.

PowerPoint remains the go-to format when I give talks around the world but I have learned that simplicity is vital from the get-go if I want to hold and retain interest. I cannot for one second presume that I have the audience's attention because guess what? They are in a world where *everyone* is vying for their attention (it's called the Attention Economy). As I said in the beginning of this book, I began to test out the best way to present my information and found that sharing my concept of Hexagon Action with actual hexagons really worked. It is not cluttered. Or complicated. It lets my points speak up and stand up for themselves. The complicated part, selecting and curating those words, has been done on my own time, toiling away.

But by the time I get in front of an audience, I need to focus not on what I put in but also, what I am prepared to leave out.

So the Simplicity Principle helps you home in unapologetically on what you can ditch in order to get real and *keep it real*. There is only so much attention out there. And only so much time. And only so much anyone can remember.

Remember

The Six-Day War

A friend of mine once stood in the middle of Piccadilly Circus yelling: 'What was the date of the Six-Day War?' This was not a general knowledge quiz; she needed the exact date. Why? Because it was her bank PIN number (the answer? 1967). Today, most of us are lucky to remember our security numbers because we have so many, and even when we do, we live in fear of cyber-theft and compromise. Here's another number six for you: the $6 trillion cost of cybercrime estimated before this century reaches adulthood and turns to 2021. We're stuck on something of an endless wheel of anxiety about keeping safe the increasing numbers we have to keep from being hacked.

Of course there is no six-day war on keeping our data safe, but a 24/7 one. One of the most obvious ways in which complexity makes our lives difficult is in the way we have all become dependent and reliant on different electronic systems, passwords, operating software and so on. As the author of *The Overflowing Brain*, Torkel Klingberg, puts it so well: 'We should be concerned about an increasingly excessive and overlapping flow of information that leaves the average member of our species increasingly distracted and disoriented.'

Although there is such a thing as good stress – called *eustress* – I personally find managing digital data overload one of the most bad-stresses around. I can feel my heart rate jump when I find myself searching for logins, or unable to download something which worked fine on my laptop but doesn't on my tablet. Thanks to cloud storage the question of finding where I have hidden passwords has reduced, but then the number of passwords required has increased, as has the worry that unless you have a different one for everything, when do you know if one of your accounts hasn't been compromised?

All of which means that we urgently need fresh strategies to cope at a very practical level with the question of memory. Keeping things simple is an obvious antidote. More devices, more platforms, more software programs, more upgrades, more passcodes is a recipe for stress of the bad kind. The high blood pressure kind. Please keep in mind the question of working memory and how finite it is. So this does mean limiting the number of passwords to the perfect six or less and to really asking whether you are putting too much pressure on your memory for it to simply cope? Although research by Alzheimer's campaigners has shown that there are a number of stressful situations in life which can trigger responses similar to actual Alzheimer's – such as long-term unemployment, debt, or sexual assault – research also shows that overloading the brain by constant 'task-switching' causes similar brain stress responses. Using fMRI – functional magnetic resonance imaging – to study brain activity in real time, researchers at the Department of Psychiatry at Yale found that:

> Overloading the working memory system was associated with varying degrees of subsequent decline in performance accuracy and reduced activation of brain regions central to both task performance and suppression of negative affect.[23]

In other words: you just can't cope with too much information. Not only will you not remember it, you will be stressed out and not remember it.

FUHGEDDABOUDIT

I love the word *fuhgeddaboudit* in which I hear the New York twang of Robert De Niro in gangster movies. Anyway, according to Urban Dictionary it means: 'Forget about it – the issue is not worth the time, energy, mental effort, or emotional resources.' I decided a while ago that if I had to try very hard to remember something it might be because I either did not want to, did not need to, or had to find a workaround. In which case, I needed to fuhgeddaboudit. You could say it is a perfect catchphrase for the Simplicity Principle along with KISS (Keep It Simple, Sweetie).

Don't think you have to stuff more and more in your head. Instead, trust yourself that you will in fact remember what you need to. Trees and bees remember how to do stuff. Our bodies 'remember' experiences. I distinctly remember the experience of going into labour with my second child and having a moment of simultaneously thinking and feeling, which went something like this: 'Oh, I remember. This is what it feels like. I know what is going to happen next.' You may think this is obvious, but I had a very complicated birth with our first child and did not think I would remember much about it. I spent two days being induced with our second child and so had assumed that the experience would be pretty different. But an ancient physical memory was triggered and then my body (closely followed by my brain) did in fact know. It remembered. You always remember your children's births of course, and their birthdays. Our second child, Anoushka, did have a memorable one which is simplicity and symmetry combined: 01.01.01. When giving it in countries that write the day and month the other way round, for example, it stays unambiguous. As it happens, the first of January is also the 'birthday' you are most likely to be assigned if you arrive as a refugee in a new country without having proof of your date of birth. I am the daughter of émigrés and I enjoy the shared milestone birthday our daughter has. And it is not hard to remember!

The Complexity Curveball

Complexity can be basic enough – a bit of form filling – but it can still throw curveballs. Apple had to issue a warning to users of older models when daylight saving hours came into force in Europe one year because an aspect of its programme had a glitch which meant to all effects and purposes it could not remember how to connect online if this change was not made manually. Or something like that: even the explanation sounds complicated! But computer memory is even worse sometimes than the human kind. Microsoft has aggravated its customers for years with updates which means its Outlook memory changes. You can search on one device and find a different result from another. Maddening. I call this kind of thing the 'Complexity Curveball' because just when you are least expecting or needing it, a huge electronic spanner can get thrown into the works. Somehow it feels worse because we are always being told by software designers and our digital brands how simple and straightforward things are (remember: simplicity sells).

Using curves in geometry is interesting for us Hexagon aficionados because it represents a deviation from the straight lines we know and love. A curveball is the unexpected. I think that the people around us who revel in complexity, who look at us and shake their heads sadly and say 'All of this simplicity is all very well, but really, life is just a bit more complicated than that, don't you think?' need to recognize that complexity is one giant curveball. The more you do, the more complicated you make things. Complexity Curveballs create unintended consequences, and make you deviate from your route. There is no simpler way to put it. If you have to remember more, and your brain can't accommodate it beyond using every training possible – and this book is suggesting the six ways which should all help you achieve more for less energy – then you might just need to *let go*.

This means trying to remember less, store less, connect to less and remember one thing: look after our internal computer, that complex, messy, muddled, limited, magnificent object in our heads. Just that one thing.

SIX
FIX

KNOWLEDGE

1 **Prioritize trust.** To decipher fact from fiction, try and keep it simple. Start by asking whether there is more to it than meets the eye – are you being wilfully blind because you want to believe it? Step back: can you trace the source of the knowledge and can you trust it?

2 **Use your antennae.** Wisdom combines experience, feeling and knowledge. Be the bee in this: use your antennae. Use your sixth sense. Bring this to the table, either the boardroom table or the coffee counter or the meeting room. Bring what you *know already*.

3 **Look for Known Unknowns.** Imagine and anticipate the Known Unknowns if you can. Accept that there are Known Unknowns... but don't be caught out by ignoring the possibility of one you might be able to do something about after all.

4 **Join the soft skills revolution.** Brush up on your hard skills and technical skills but don't neglect the soft ones. Can you negotiate well, hold a conversation well, show your empathy?

5 **Use a Knowledge Dashboard.** Cut through the fatty tissue of TMI (too much information) while also providing variety and diversity, crucial ingredients for Social Health as well as physical health.

6 **Avoid Complexity Curveballs.** Keep focus on what you need to know and can remember (don't exceed your cognitive load) rather than throwing yourself Complexity Curveballs.

8

Side 5: Networks

Diverse networks matter more than networking

Populate your life with people different from you. Once you leave school, you get to choose the kinds of people you're going to be around rather than forced to be around them.[1]

KUMAIL NANJANI IN A COLLEGE COMMENCEMENT ADDRESS

The human species is a social one. Who we live and work with, who we like or dislike, how we communicate about each other is all done using our social skills, including language and culture. We show, we share, we show off, all in ways which are simple reflections of deeply complex social cues. Yet we humans are fundamentally simple in our basic need to be connected to each other. Once we have food, shelter, safety, we need love to survive.

The neuroscientist Matthew Lieberman has shown that the human brain has a permanent motor running which concerns itself, always, with its social experiences.[2] His research has been able to demonstrate that we experience loss and emotional anguish very much like pain itself. It is not surprising that technology has given the human race social networks because we existed on them all the time before the digital world came along. Humans have made social networks in real time ever since time began. Therefore it is not surprising that we communicate on social networks very greedily. Just at the time of writing, 60 billion messages are exchanged each day on the Facebook Messenger and WhatsApp platforms alone. The clever designers of algorithms who feed our brain chemistry with dopamine hits have figured out awesome ways to replicate our natural needs, electronically. GlobalWebIndex reports that the average social media user now spends 2 hours 16 minutes each day on social platforms, which equates to roughly one-third of their total internet time, and one-seventh of their waking lives.[3]

In this chapter I hope to help you regain the balance between the networks you keep online and offline and begin to appreciate the crucial difference between networking, a rather human and contrived way to connect with others, and understanding networks themselves. There is a big difference! Networks reflect the very essence of nature, and of the Hexagon Action way of connected patterns. Pretty much everything, including people, is governed by laws of networks. Our transport and infrastructure is all built on networks which mirror the natural world's network structures from trees to hexagon-shaped crystals in chemistry (copper, gold, lead, silver are among the metals we build from which all have hexagon-shaped elemental structures). Trees illustrate perfectly what is called network effects. On the surface a forest is thousands of individual trees but underneath they are all connected by a network of interconnected roots. The German 'tree whisperer' Peter Wohlleben, whose research about tree networks is shaking up the scientific community, has uncovered in his book *The Hidden Life of Trees* that trees depend on a network of relations which are remarkably relatable to us.[4]

In this respect trees can be called social and yet of course they are not animals. So one of the reasons why honey bees are the poster-species for simplicity is that they are themselves social creatures: despite being so tiny, so apparently wordless, they communicate with each other and build lives together in ways we can recognize and relate to. Bees use whatever technology is available – their antennae are hugely sophisticated natural sensors – in order to communicate with each other, but never at the expense of being together in person. Or perhaps I should say, *in bee*. The idea of being the bee, and indeed of building and belonging, is core to the Simplicity Principle as I have explained earlier.

In this section the networks of Hexagon Action take inspiration quite a bit from bees, going beyond what is normally thought of as networking and focusing more on what we know about the natural science of networks themselves:

1 **Hierarchy of communication:** using all six senses when communicating

2 **Superorganism:** the social species that we are

3 **Networks:** networks in the workplace are vital

4 **Social capital:** avoid echo chambers for more equality

5 **Salons:** old coffee-houses in new coffee shops

6 **Social Six:** who to count on matters most

Hierarchy of communication

Keep it real

You may not feel it is appropriate to associate love with, say, your boss, or your co-worker, or your roommate, but substitute that word for 'connection' and you might get the picture. We have to be connected to others, or we don't perform well as humans. The role of prison is to exclude a criminal from society itself, from family, from friends, as the very essence of the punishment. And 'solitary confinement' is the worst level of sanction a prisoner gets if they misbehave: to be totally alone is understood universally as being very tough on us humans.

Actually, being social is a basic form of survival. Through image scanning of brain activity Professor Lieberman discovered three half-a-hexagon's worth of key neural networks which put our connectedness at the centre of our cognitive senses, from 1) registering social pain and pleasure, to 2) reading emotions and predicting behaviour, and 3) our cultural beliefs and norms. As he says in his book *Social*: 'Being socially connected is a need with a capital N.'

I developed my Hierarchy of Communication model to keep us focused on exactly how much time we do and don't spend connecting in real time with real people (remembering that it is important to *keep it real*).[5] Yes, you can reach many people if you broadcast on social media, and gain 'likes', 'shares' and 'comments' but this is not the same as using your senses to physically see, smell, touch or hear another person, or taste them (or taste food with them). And of course social media is very bad for the sixth sense, in that it is super hard to use your instinct online: a comment or post or email is a very blunt instrument.

The Hierarchy of Communication is simple. Imagine a pyramid with the top being the most exclusive and valuable form and the bottom the least.

On top: Face-to-face
in person or by voice-to-voice

Middle: Written/drawn
a sent communication, by snail mail,
email or on a social platform

Bottom: Broadcast
a mass form of communication, using
mailing systems such as Mailchimp or
via the social networks themselves

Being face-to-face in a Facebook world

Even though it is much more time-consuming to do things face-to-face, and even though you obviously reach fewer people doing it, this is where the real value lies: being face-to-face in a Facebook world. I am going to be straight with you when I say that although I recognize the benefits of social media, and am an avid user myself, I think it is an inferior medium to being in a room with a person, face-to-face. The evolutionary psychologist Robin Dunbar of the University of Oxford is a man who has a number named after him: Dunbar's Number. This is because his research has shown consistently that the maximum number of relationships humans can have at any given time is around 150. I went to talk to Robin at his book-crammed office in Oxford for a BBC radio series I wrote and presented called *Networking Nations*. He had done some recent research specifically around social media versus face-to-face and said:

> Social media certainly helps to slow down the natural rate of decay in relationship quality that would set in once we cannot readily meet friends face-to-face. But no amount of social media will prevent a friend eventually becoming 'just another acquaintance' if you don't meet face-to-face from time to time. There is something paramount about face-to-face interactions that is crucial for maintaining friendships. Seeing the white of their eyes from time to time seems to be crucial to the way we maintain friendships.[6]

There is another clear benefit to being physically in the same space: being physical. For instance, research shows that touch, and especially a hug, is amazingly powerful at reducing stress and building trust.[7] You may not imagine that giving a hug in the boardroom is a good idea, or touching the arm of someone who is your senior, but it absolutely is: physical connection which obviously cannot happen online is the magic recipe, the most human thing you can do in a machine age. If you can observe the Hierarchy of Communication, it means using the essence of the Simplicity Principle: **keep it simple** and **keep close to nature**. No filter, as they say on Instagram. The problem with being online so much is that it takes a lot of time, energy and strategy to just *cope* (if you don't want to get sucked in to being online *all* the time). And that energy, time and strategy could be better used elsewhere. To coin the phrase 'be your best self', the human is a pretty incredible self to be, if you let that social self be shown fully.

Superorganism

The best cross-pollinators in the world

Let's take a step back from the nuts and bolts of email and social networks for a moment, back into the natural world. Biologists call humans and our fellow social species the honey bees superorganisms, which means that we cooperate with each other and are socially entwined. That is, we live, work, communicate with each other and we create, build and make stuff together.

The entire bee species (all 25,000 varieties) was declared the most important species on the planet by the Royal Geographical Society because of its role in pollination of plants and flowers. The ability to dip in and out of different sources of pollen spreads through nature's network effects what plants need to grow. Quite apart from the life-sustaining reality of pollination, there is daily life's enhancements. The biologist and conservationist Thor Hanson, who wrote an excellent book about bees called *Buzz*,[8] analysed a McDonald's Big Mac and concluded that almost every single ingredient relied on pollination from bees: from the paprika which goes into the sauce to the iceberg lettuce, everything except the bun and the beef was related to bee pollination. Imagine eating a hamburger with no seasoning or added natural ingredients other than pure meat or grain: McDonald's knows how to satisfy your taste buds. His point is that over 150 crops require or benefit from pollination, without which much of what we taste would be rather dull and boring.

Cross-pollination is also a classic example of network effects, how things like, well, pollen, spread. I like to think of humans as being great cross-pollinators too. We spread ideas, values, culture, language, and traditions. If we did not share in this way we could not build a world. Thanks to social sharing and cross-pollination of ideas, specifically the generosity of Herminia Ibarra, the Charles Handy Professor of Organizational Behaviour at The London Business School, she directed me to her fellow academic Selin Kesebir's paper on just this topic. *The Superorganism*

Account of Human Sociality: How and when human groups are like beehives points out that 'At any level of organization, consolidating power by cooperating with other units at the same level may lead to a huge competitive advantage' and that like bees, 'Human beings are extraordinary collaborators, able to undertake collective actions involving thousands or even millions of people.'[9]

Of course staying close to nature's geometry and pattern is core to both the Simplicity Principle and the technique of Hexagon Action. The underlying structures of nature's networks from bees to trees illustrate the power of connected, collaborative behaviour. Here is a very good human illustration of this in action too.

The Wild Boars

In Thailand back in the summer of 2018 the eyes of the world were fixed on the Tham Luang cave system in Thailand, near the border with Myanmar. Trapped on a rock ledge deep inside was the Wild Boars soccer team of 12 boys and their coach, who had ventured into the caves about two weeks earlier. It was monsoon season. Water was rising and oxygen levels falling. Not all of the boys could even swim. Time was running out. Everyone feared the worst. What saved the boys was a perfect example of a human superorganism, of a team which came together naturally and which worked around nature's complexity to find a simple solution. They succeeded. The boys came out alive.

The Thai Cave Rescue was a stunning example of what physicist Albert-László Barabási calls 'scale-free-networks' – networks that keep replicating and getting bigger.[10] In 10 days, the network that helped rescue the boys had swelled to 10,000 people from more than 20 nations. They had skills including meditation (to calm the boys), medicine, and rock climbing; and there were experts from armies, navies, and caving. The network deployed both cutting-edge new tech, such as drones, sonar scanners, and mesh technology radios operating on multiple frequencies, and old-fashioned caving 'Hey Phones' from the 1970s used in caving. And the oldest technology of all: the organizing skills of the superorganism.

Networks that come together like this and use technology, community, and communications in a timely manner are an example of the UN's 'Leave No One Behind' strategy for achieving sustainable development goals. I consider it an example of Social Health in action. These humans connected with each other, using the technology available, to harness the critical three elements I call 'The Knot' in which the right Knowledge, added to the right Networks, in the right Timeframe helped to get everyone out safely, within the deadline of rising water and falling oxygen.

The boys were pulled through the caves using pulleys installed by experienced local rock climbers. They were sedated and alternately carried, slid, and ziplined over and sometimes even under the treacherous rising water. Wild Boars were saved by superorganism behaviour. It's such an inspiring story!

Networks

Working the room

For decades I have worked in the field of social networking, the kind that takes place in real rooms not chat rooms, and when I was made Honorary Visiting Professor in Networking at London's Cass Business School it was a world first. At the time I regarded it as a small victory for the idea of face-to-face networking in a social network world, not least because for years a number of people had begun to believe that social networks would eliminate the need for anything else. Of course nothing could be further from the truth. Research in the *Journal of Experimental Psychology* showed that you are 34 times more likely to get what you ask for if you ask in person rather than by email.[11] Suspicion and lack of empathy are all factors in this, but also over-optimism by those sending the email. This tells me that we have really drunk too much Kool-Aid when it comes to thinking that electronic net-worked ways of reaching out to people are better than the in-person kind.

The difficulty is that so much of what is called networking is incredibly difficult to do, not half as much fun as people say it is, and therefore people prefer to hide behind screen-based network-ing instead. What's the problem? Well, in a word, shyness. It wasn't that long ago that many of us wore uniforms to work. Some of us still do, of course, particularly on factory or shop floors. But most of us dress down. But having a uniform can feel like both an identity and a protection. When your company sends you out to a 'networking event' it can feel very exposing. Like you have to be an all-singing and all-dancing salesperson, when in fact you might just want to hang out in the corner of the room (I have had many such experiences myself, despite being technically an extrovert). It is human to feel shy. Even if you are someone who feels entirely comfortable socially and loves the idea of working the room, what does success look like, other than having a nice time? It's never really clear. Networking has never stopped feeling like a code you can't crack for many people and think we have to start to talk and think very differ-ently about it at work.

The best way to think about networking is to avoid thinking about it in transactional terms – *what can I get out of it* – and instead think of it in terms of relationships: *how can I forge a connection with someone?* Believe me, this difference is crucial. And borrow a leaf from another part of the forest, the chapter on knowledge and Curation: be very, very selective about the 'room' you choose to go in. Your time is precious, and I would even go so far as to say you should consciously avoid going to anything which advertises itself as having 'networking drinks' or 'networking time'. That's a real giveaway about the transactional, not relational mindset. Any event which invites you to attend because you might be welcome, and because it hopes to be interesting, well, think about making time for that. Networks will flow automatically from an event organized to prioritize people and content. It may seem like a minor detail but trust me, understanding the difference between networking and networks is really important in work.

Power to the peoplebase

Let's go back to love, and Matthew Lieberman's research that the human being's brain is concerned first and foremost with it. The dictionary definition of relationship includes 'being related or interrelated'. In other words, being in some kind of network, from the familial kind of having relatives, to all the other kinds of relationships. Including work. Once you start to think of where you work and who you work with as a set of relationships, then you might begin to value nurturing them in a very different way. In a more personal way.

In order for this to happen, perhaps a good starting point is to look beyond the office relationships and dynamics, important though they are, and into the hidden stack of relationships which live digitally, in that no man's land known as 'the database'. Anyone who has run a business or been involved in marketing or sales will have had a *lot* to do with databases. They have barely modernized at all in 50 years. They get bigger and better at 'data capture' but the people who make, sell and usually manage the systems run the risk of focusing less on the Simplicity Principle and more on the magic of complexity. That the more a database can *do* with its data, the better.

When you think about it, putting the names of people into an electronic system to manage communicating may seem simple enough, but is it personal? I am old enough to remember the Rolodex, a wonderful index-card holder to record information about anything but especially people, invented in the 1950s by the Danish engineer Hildaur Neilsen. At the height of its popularity, before the internet age, 10 million Rolodexes were sold each year. I miss them. I could see and count and touch the cards, which kept me connected quite literally to them. Today my contacts live on LinkedIn, and in my office database system, and on my Outlook, and on Facebook and my other social networks. It's not the same. There are many more of them, but it is hard to keep track. It is much more complicated. The scale of technology allows us to record many millions of human beings, but what has that got to do with relating to or communicating with them? Not much in reality.

Let's go back to nature and to trees: We now know just how networked trees in a forest are, thanks to the groundbreaking work of Peter Wohlleben, shared in his book *The Hidden Life of Trees*. A forest is a giant network above ground and below ground. It has to constantly renew itself. Deciduous trees shed their leaves each winter to protect themselves from being blown away by harsh winds. Producing new leaves is worth the energy if it ensures survival. How much fresh energy do we ever bring to the systems which manage our own forest floor of connections? Not nearly enough.

Small is beautiful

Finally, a word about scale in networks at work. It isn't just that bigger is not better in terms of conferences or events or databases, but in terms of getting anything done. The Simplicity Principle rule is, quite simply, avoid a meeting or email list with more than six people in it, but as a general rule the size and scale of anything makes a massive difference to outcome.

The management theorist Frederic Laloux identified what he calls the 'Teal Organization'.[12] In this theory, successful organizations succeed by avoiding traditional models of leadership and relying instead on collective self-management and functioning through collaboration in small units. Laloux writes about self-managing, 'no boss' cultures in which teams are tiny – perhaps 10 to 12 people – which makes them very flexible and able to adapt quickly. The US human capital management software firm Kronos has a boss – Aron Ain – who pointedly describes himself as an 'un-leader', even though it is a billion-plus dollar business and has over 6,000 employees worldwide. In his book *Work Inspired* he relates the story of 'Project Falcon', developed by a dedicated team of 25 people, charged with doing something different. As he relates, 'Our workforce was highly engaged. Our customers were happy. And yet, some of us were worried. We wanted to guarantee future success and decided to take proactive measures.' This tiny team was allowed to experiment and explore, and this fledgling project eventually became a product called Workforce Dimensions which went on to reach No 1 in independent research rankings of workforce management solutions in 2019, with a top-rated product score of 95 per cent. The power of small.

Social capital

Who you know and what you know

When I started my network business, Editorial Intelligence, back in 2005, I wanted to bring together two kinds of people who were at opposite ends of the spectrum (in their own eyes anyway): journalists and PRs. The strapline I gave the company at the time was 'Where PR Meets Journalism'. I had previously been a book PR (hence meeting Maya Angelou) and had managed to build up a good set of relationships with journalists, and possibly even their respect, which is notoriously difficult as there is a hidden law that they are way above the moral food chain when it comes to PR.

All of this was back in the analogue era, the days of the 'long liquid lunch' in London, when even fairly junior and young women like me could go out to swish restaurants on expenses to exchange news and gossip and build contacts. I remember having sushi in Farringdon with the young Alan Rusbridger, who went on to become editor of *The Guardian*, and I am still in touch with many of the journalists from that time. One or two have become good friends. How did I have the confidence to connect with them in the first place? Well, I had Social Capital.

Social capital is the strength of connections. If you have no social capital, you can't access 'value' in the community: you can't get things done or get on. It's a term borrowed from economics and is slightly slippery, but over the years it has built up to become something people accept means: your network matters. In the UK in those days, the media all knew my surname thanks to my father reaching the height of his academic fame just as my career took off. Everyone knew the name Hobsbawm and so when I asked if I could go and see people, they said yes. Just like financial capital, the more you have to begin with the better. I could tell you sincerely that all the things I have written about here such as curiosity and motivation have helped me and all of that is true. But social capital is a wealth I began with and I have always wanted others to have the same benefit.

But how? The network at Editorial Intelligence quickly outran the confines of media and PR and we began to expand into connecting people in politics, science, technology, business and still PR and journalism with each other. But I noticed that everyone was senior in some way (otherwise they couldn't afford our membership) and it was still way before today's consciousness about diversity of race and class opened up the closed world of 'the professions'. I felt this was wrong morally, but the more I read about network science, the more I realized this was also stupid tactically. Because when you look at the studies of social connections, or the way in which network effects grow and spread, you a realize that good strong networks thrive on diversity. They require it. Whether it's a rumour or a cold, networks rely on something or someone acting as the hub or node, and the strength and number of connections they have so that the thing, whatever it is, can jump and connect between them. Like our friend the bee, buzzing between one flower and another. Spreading.

I was still puzzling this problem when I attended a very early morning breakfast meeting in a big government building with senior people. As I checked in my coat I noticed – remember the importance of noticing – that the young woman on the coat-check looked dejected, and way too young to be spending the start of her life not really being noticed by many. I started talking to her a bit, and discovered that she was a graduate. She had no connections. She had no confidence. She gave out a very lost vibe. I asked her if she would like to come and work for me for a bit to try out my office as an alternative to the coat-check room and she agreed.

But this particular story doesn't have a happy ending. Marice did come and work with me, but I quickly realized that she had never had the opportunity to develop her soft skills, and that somehow going to university was supposed to give her confidence and good job prospects, but it wasn't enough. I realized we needed to help nurture confidence and connection, not just provide raw opportunity. Out of this experience we began to experiment with a much more ambitious social capital project, where we matched our members, oozing confidence and careers, with young Londoners like Marice, over a much longer period of time than just a paid internship. We started to explore what happened to both sides of the coin, the 'scholar' as we called the young 'uns, and the mentors. And guess what? Really productive, happy, creative connections were made. The diversity and cross-pollination of people worked beautifully.

Today we run a network-within-a-network, called The Social Capital network. The structure is simple, symmetrical, geometric: we match one scholar with three of our network members over the course of the year and ask the mentors to share two or three full or half-days of whatever they are doing, so that these soft skills build social capital. The network is partly run by Shanice Shields-Mills, our first scholar. She came to our attention because she had turned the difficulties on her housing estate into triumph, through an instinctive understanding of the power of social capital and the force of a very considerable personality. Shanice had turned adversity into opportunity and she had attracted the interest of the main London newspaper, the *Evening Standard*. In turn, a senior executive at the investment bank Citi who sponsored social inclusion initiatives with the newspapers spotted her potential, and introduced her to an intern programme run by someone she knew elsewhere in the communications world. Both of these executives knew us. By now the motto of this story should be clear. Cross-pollination works. Build value in communities. Have true diversity around you. Help others. Use networks.

Salons

Whatever the topic, the main business of coffee-houses was the sharing and discussion of news and opinion in spoken, written and printed form; their patrons wanted to imbibe information as well as coffee and tobacco.[13]

TOM STANDAGE

The coffee melting pot

The world drinks more than 10 million tons of it a year with Finland topping the polls for drinking the most, closely followed by Sweden and Iceland. According to the International Coffee Organization, the United States and UK rank below Switzerland, Greece and Germany, but all of these nations drink the most. I confess that I am a bit of a coffee addict myself. I like very strong continental espresso beans, ground and then made on a stovetop pot. Like everyone, I associate coffee with conversation. They have always gone together. Back in the 17th century, the coffee-house became famous as a diverse meeting and melting pot of ideas in London. In his book about social media's history the *Economist* journalist Tom Standage says that coffee shops were a kind of real-time social media.

He quotes a fantastic pamphlet called *The Character of a Coffee-House*, published in 1673 (when social media definitely meant conveying rumour, news and opinion in person only): 'The room stinks of tobacco worse than hell of brimstone, and is as full of smoke as their heads that frequent it.'

Today's coffee shops don't have communal tables for people to exchange news and views like a trading floor, and more's the pity. Today you are most likely to see a coffee shop with little conversation but lots of tap-tapping of laptops. Yet the 17th-century habit of conversation, also known as the salon, badly needs to be reinvented here in the 21st century, because there is no better way to build and nurture networks than through it. The historian Simon Schama once paid me the highest of compliments (I thought) when he called me a *salonnière* in reference to the women – and it *was* women – who used to hold salons in grand private homes in France around the same time that a grubbier version of conversation and ideas was happening in the coffee-houses springing up across Europe's great cities.

Quitting conferences

I became, by accident and without planning to, a professional salonnière of sorts, simply by my upbringing and personality. Although I definitely experience shyness like everyone does, I am certainly on the extrovert end of the spectrum: more outgoing than not. As I child I watched my parents convene regular informal supper parties at their house and watched my grandmother do the same in her apartment. There was food, laughter, conversation, argument. People were passionate, friendly, and different from each other, even though they had things in common too. I used to get paid a little bit of pocket money to wash dishes for my parents but ended up hovering to hear the stories, the laughter, and to soak up the atmosphere of writers, thinkers, artists who used to visit our house back in the 1970s. For a decade in my current business I ran a kind of moving coffee-house salon, a conference called 'Names

Not Numbers', which convened an equally oddball group. The point about salons is that they are great equalizers. I have a photo of the woman who had connected us with Shanice, our brilliant scholar, face-to-face with Margaret Atwood who spoke one year and who loved it. I paired her with a brilliant insect expert called Bridget Nicholls and afterwards Atwood gave Names Not Numbers the highest praise, calling it 'a great cross-pollination of ideas'.

The conference business, which always sells itself 'with networking drinks', tries to persuade people that it really is a giant salon, and to some extent, but only some extent, that's true. Certainly the conference business is big: $30 billion dollars is the size of the conference events industry. Countries compete for conference business. Germany has the largest capacity venue anywhere in the world, stretching to half-a-million square metres, and a third of people who attend conferences go to events with more than 2,500 people. That may be to justify the cost of sending someone, and the time–cost of attending, but it doesn't quite work in comparison with the Dunbar Number of 150 relationships, or my Hierarchy of Communication that you need to be face-to-face in small groups either. No, the conference business may be a good way of selling things, with some useful network-making on the side, but if you really want to build networks, you need smaller salons.

Marnita's Table

I would define a salon as a curated gathering with small enough groups that everyone can be seen and heard and remembered. I came across a really inspiring woman called Marnita Shroedl in Minneapolis who founded an organization called Marnita's Table which 'exists to increase equality and decrease disparities across distance'.[14] They practise what they call 'radical hospitality' by bringing together groups who are often in disagreement with each other but who, through shared discussion, over a meal, find a way through that difference. I had a long phone call with Marnita about the way she has developed a really unique blend of the salon, social capital programming, and change. I love the way that Marnita's Table holds galas called 'Start the Conversation' at which they raise funds by inviting you to 'get out of your bubble... engage with decision-makers, community leaders and family members and share a delicious cross-cultural feast'.

The truth is that the idea of salons is very much one of Hexagon Action. It is about containment and geometry (small, shaped, structured). Salons cross-pollinate people and ideas. Knowledge flows through them in rather a timely manner. And trust develops. So very much like the way one hexagon joins another and then another: organic, natural, rather magical.

Complexity junkies, those people who always want scale and speed over slow and pared-down, love big, impersonal conferences. But the question is, do you really? And if you don't, how can you create your alternative? Well, if you belong to a book group, you are already in a salon. And if you organize a meet-up, that counts too. A meal out with friends? Yes, that's a salon. Take the coffee-house rather than the conference approach and embrace more of what you are probably doing without even realizing: find your salon or become a salonnière.

Social Six

The last section here may seem obvious, given that I have already set out the stall for the number six, but given how many people we are connected to, it can be tough to identify the six or so people in your networks who really matter to you at any given time. When was the last time you thought about it? Perhaps, like me, you find yourself caught up instead in an endless round of communication, by email, in meetings, at salons or conferences and never really stop to think 'what's my personal people base'? This section is all about why you should stop, take stock, and identify your very own Social Six.

The kitchen cabinet

We think of the political circle of advisers known as the 'kitchen cabinet' and everyone should have one. The very idea of having a large crowd-sourced group of advisers is different to a small, trusted and intimate one. There's a funny story in Britain about the time when a large crowd turned into something like a small circle of 'kitchen cabinet' advisers. In an online poll about naming a ship operated by the British Antarctic Survey, the hashtag #nameourshippoll resulted in a surge of name nominations and the winner was rather an odd name for such a prestigious ship: *Boaty McBoatface*. The politician in charge had to do an about-face and renamed the ship something grand and let the crowd-sourced name apply to one of its submarines. Be careful what you wish for! But this is a serious example of how, if you let too wide a circle into something which requires a bit of serious strategic thinking, things can get complicated. No, a kitchen cabinet, which I'm renaming 'the Social Six', is a much better idea.

The perfect number

Let's recap: six is a mathematically 'perfect' number, present in a surprisingly large swathe of cultural and scientific contexts. So perhaps most of all, it falls under the maximum limit of our working memory (seven items) and therefore is a highly practical number. Hexagon Action is all about 'Keeping it real' after all.

It doesn't have to be absolutely literal. If you have a board of eight or a family of nine these are all good numbers too, of course. But it is about thinking that when you want to get things done, or when you want to count on people, once you start stretching beyond six it is just unlikely to be that meaningful or helpful.

In terms of organizing perfectly, the number six has a symmetry which matters. People often list, label and organize priorities in threes, and 3, along with 2 and 1, is a factor of 6. Corporate fundraisers talk about boards being divided into thirds: one-third active, one-third passive and one-third not useful at all. This may seem a bit harsh, but anyone who has ever sat on a board or been part of a large group knows that the active and useful people often surface as a much smaller number than the whole. In other words, you don't have to start with six, but don't assume more than six will be getting stuck in!

Taking stock

The idea of your Social Six harks back to Clarity. If you want to get something done, you need to make a decision. Who helps you decide? Or who can you count on to implement that decision? We meet many thousands of people in our lives. The average life expectancy for women is 75 and for men is 70, and we tend to start remembering who we meet meaningfully from the age of five. Even being conservative in our estimation, and imagining that over the course of a life we meet the same small number of people each day (rather than a lot at a certain time and less as we age), it is reasonable to assume we all meet between 500 and 1,000 people a year, so around 50,000 people at least. But we can't possibly count on them, any more than at a conference we can do meaningful 'networking' with them . Thinking about your Social Six is a way of taking a key snapshot of your life as it is now, and who is in it. This helps you decide and get Clarity, and it also helps you figure out who to trust for information, and who you can really be yourself with. It isn't necessarily a single list of six, but several. Who is your Social Six amongst colleagues, family, friends? Who is your Social Six at your kids' school, and so on.

You can probably guess what I will say next: try it. Make a six-list and see.

SIX FIX

NETWORKS

1 **Be face-to-face in a Facebook world.** The Hierarchy of Communication keeps us focused on how much time we do and don't spend connecting with people in real life, and of the value of keeping it natural: face-to-face. Be honest, are you hiding behind screen-based networks? Though it may be much more time-consuming, face-to-face is where the real value lies. It also forces you to prioritize and focus on what matters most.

2 **Think peoplebase not database.** Remember that everyone wants to be a name, not a number. Organize who you know and how you communicate not based on quantity of relationships, but quality.

3 **Networks, not networking.** The best way to think about networking is to adopt a relational not transactional mindset. Think not *what can I get out of it?* but *how can I forge a connection with someone?* Networks will flow from (smaller) events organized to prioritize people and content.

4 **Be social.** Create social capital by being part of communities, because it strengthens them and it strengthens you. Like bees we thrive on shared specialized knowledge and draw on swarm intelligence to make better decisions.

5 **Coffee-houses not conferences.** Recreate the salon and the coffee-house in small, intimate gatherings, and don't think that a large conference is a good substitute. They are different.

6 **Social Six.** Take stock, and identify your 'social six'. Who are the six or so people in your networks who really matter to you now, and on whom you can count when you need to get things done.

9

Side 6: Time

Treat your time like your body

*For all the compasses in the world, there's only one direction,
and time is its only measure.*
TOM STOPPARD, *ROSENCRANTZ AND GUILDENSTERN ARE DEAD*

We can't stretch time. When I ask students or people in an audience what the number 168 means they often look blank. It is the number of hours in the week. It is almost as if we have become so in thrall to large numbers of data and digital limitlessness that a small, fixed number feels confusing – and way too small. But it's the reality. The complexity of modern life eats into time, rather than keeping things simple. Research shows that the average internet user spends six hours a day online.[1] Our time is spent zigzagging across a complex set of tasks including communication (250 billion emails are exchanged daily around the world), search (5 billion Google searches per day), shopping (we're spending more than $3.5 trillion dollars annually across the world on the internet).[2] That is before you count the time we spend on social media and before you count the time we do other things like walk, talk, commute, eat, and sleep. Yes, the way we spend time is often that of a helpless bystander as the egg-timer trickles the sand down in front of our eyes. So this sixth and final side to simplicity is all about this most precious commodity and the axiom is simple: 'Treat your time like your body.' And because time is short, this section will be too – deliberately so!

The Simplicity Principle aims to help you make the most of time, by focusing on what happens to it. We cannot stop the meter running, inside or outside our bodies, but we can control how we approach the very question of time, and simplify it by considering:

1 **Deadline:** keep control of deadline and timeline

2 **Schedule:** be the gatekeeper of your time

3 **Time Zones:** how to work in global villages

4 **Interruption:** setting boundaries often and keeping them

5 **Body clock:** finding the best time to suit you

6 **Past and Present:** there is no time like now

Deadline

It's extremely hard to discover the truth when you are ruling the world. You are just far too busy.[3]

YUVAL NOAH HARARI

The quarterly result

Douglas Adams said that he loved deadlines: 'I love the whooshing noise they make as they go by.' I think the world divides into those who keep deadlines and those who don't. Like people who are always late and those who keep to time. Keeping to time, holding on to it, matters a lot. And deadlines are important because they give us focus and shape. The geometric aspect of Hexagon Action is measurement and pattern. So on the whole, I like deadlines. Lots of us rely on deadlines to power us over the line and get finished. I find a deadline is often a good thing, focusing my mind on what really matters. Ask any good journalist how they work and they will usually say 'to deadline'. But many of us work all the time to deadlines which are not really in our control at all. Take the quarterly result. Businesses rely on a cycle of reporting to shareholders the status of various measurements in any given calendar quarter. Their standing on stock markets may depend on it, but the concept works across sectors and has become mainstream. In practice what this means is that a short-term mindset often creeps into how we run things when it might be better to take the long view.

In nature, the long view can be seen in our friends the trees. They too have seasonal deadlines, but the overall time frame is much, much longer. The Great Basin bristlecone pines (*Pinus longaeva*), for example, date back 4,500 years – at least.[4] The 100-year life, which for humans is finally becoming achievable thanks to science and medicine, is really at the low end for trees. They don't have quarterly results. They don't have any deadlines at all. Bees don't have specific deadlines, they have cycles, rhythms, routines. It's not the same as an unachievable fixed point that everyone has to abide by. Bees constantly adapt environmentally. Businesses and those tied to the quarterly cycle are doing something essentially un-natural, making the idea of deadline something artificial.

The next generation of purposeful leaders will recognize this and I'll know the change has happened when we see the end of quarterly reporting.

Growth stocks

What about another measurement: Growth. In the investment business, growth stock is one which is held and matures in value over time. This at least builds in fewer deadlines and more of a financial evolution. Let things take their own course. Warren Buffet often invests in stock which he can afford to see rise, fall, and rise again. We should learn from this kind of stock when we look at our own deadlines. How instant do we need our gratification to be – or how fast are we gratifying someone else's idea of success? A deadline is a form of pressure and not everyone or everything thrives under pressure. Remember the difference between 'eustress', the good time of stress, and its opposite, 'distress'. A deadline can be false, too fast, and can cause distress rather than productivity. Deadlines matter if you want to be productive and grow. You have to use judgement and some of the characteristics I have covered earlier, such as integrity, to get the best out of them.

Timeline

There is another kind of deadline to be wary of too, and that's the timeline of a corporate or a career politician. The electoral cycle as it is known often radically shapes policies which are often crunched to match politics not people. One of the reasons why politics has become so distrusted – even the United Nations chief António Guterres has talked of a 'deficit in trust' in politics – is that simplistic promises are made based on political cycles and not reality. Certain things may not take 4,500 tree-years to deliver, but they take more than several hundred days. As the thinker Seth Godin put it:

> We focus on the days, making short-term decisions, instead of being cognizant of the years. We ignore the benefits that short-term pain can have in earning us long-term satisfaction. Which means that we often fail to invest, embracing a shortcut instead.[5]

Simplicity as I see it is about what can be realistically achieved, rightly pared down and focused on. Being simplistic is where you are wildly unrealistic. So, any time you have a deadine or a timeline which suggests something not possible, or where corners get cut to achieve it, I have one word for you: avoid.

Schedule

Nobody knowingly lets someone else feed them unless they are unable to feed themselves. Yet what does happen on an everyday basis is that we lose control of our time or hand it over to others. It's called the schedule, the calendar and the diary. I find that the best way to apply the Simplicity Principle to my life is to control my time to the best of my ability. This covers when I am on- and offline, when I'm in meetings or not, and what I do with my time. I am one of the lucky ones. Not everyone can control their time and this is not just a case of 'time poverty', ie not having enough time, but of not being able to decide how to spend it.

In a famous study carried out in the 1970s, researchers gave a control group of elderly people in a care home a plant to take care of and an ability to choose movies, and compared their death rates over an 18-month period with another group who had no control over anything. I'm terribly shocked to relay that the death rate in the group with no control was *twice* as high as the one which had some degree of independence and choice.[6]

And in a work context, having greater control of time leads to higher productivity. (I define productivity not just as the dry output of product per hour but of motivation, engagement, creativity). In Sweden the Svartedalens study has shown that when you give workers control over their time by giving them a six-hour day, for instance, the amount of absenteeism from sickness and stress halves.[7] So flexibility, what I call 'flexibilism', counts every bit as clock-watching does.

Overtime

All of this means that the new wealth in life is not just money, and not just health, but time. Research done by University College London and the Finnish Institute of Occupational Health found that a tiny bit of overtime is no bad thing, but that the minute you go significantly over that, the rate of heart attacks or coronary heart disease spikes by as much as 60 per cent[8] – another indicator that when someone else controls our time we suffer. As more and more people enter the unstable job market, from zero hours to freelancing, every hour counts. So, when you decide to simplify your time, one of the first things to do is look at how your calendar is going to be shaped: what the pattern of time looks like and feels like. I never, for instance, agree to be on one side of town one hour and another side of town the next. I often have back-to-back meetings in the same place, and I try and build in a realistic amount of time for anyone I hire or work with to get what they need to do done. I'm not a fan of overtime, because it usually means you're spending someone else's time and not really paying for it. That's bad form.

Sweetening a tough gig

Everyone's work requirements are different, and if you work in a shop-floor or factory-floor environment then your scheduling issues won't be so much about meetings as about flexibility for time off. But more and more of us don't work in a fixed and scheduled environment, but in a more mixed way, with different jobs. Many of us now work in the gig economy, making our own luck. Research shows that as many as half of the US workforce is expected to be classified as freelance by 2030.[9] The World Economic Forum's *Future of Jobs* report in 2016 cited the changing nature of work and freelance working as the top trend to look out for, which shows that the United States often starts a workplace trend which other economies follow.[10] Not everyone is suited to being freelance. Being freelance is tough because not only do you have to manage distractions, but you have to manage the time you dedicate to marketing and selling yourself.

Take a cue from the bee here. Try and make whatever you spend your time on stretch as far as it can. Imagine your product is honey. Or wax. The uses range from practical to medicinal. The same ingredients get reshaped, repurposed. The time it has taken to create them gets taken by humans and made into things people enjoy and can use. The freelancer of tomorrow will be that bee: identifying their own talents and skills and creating a way of using them again and again in creative and helpful ways. They will need luck of course. And part of luck is timing. But what I mean is that, where you can control your time, use it well. If this means getting a new skill or qualification, use it. If it means doing one of Seth Godin's UDEMY online freelance courses, to get better accustomed to being your freelancer self, do that. Fit into your schedule something which is going to give you a sweet reward if you possibly can.

How to work in global villages

The world doesn't just run 365 days a year, 24/7. It has at least 24 major time zones, and additional local ones. Complicated. In Russia there are 22 time zones alone. Yikes. The way we keep track of time zones is through UTC or Coordinated Universal Time, which for age-old reasons is measured from Greenwich, London, my home town. When I wake up at home, my friends in India are entering early evening. Colleagues in South Korea and Japan are probably finishing dinner and winding down for the night, unless there is a night club involved. Which makes work these days much more complex than it used to be.

A company which specializes in the growth area of remote working has published guidelines on the etiquette of different time zones. Remote.co lists five pointers which include things like 'setting a universal time', but the one I think matters most is 'learn your co-worker's schedules'.[11] When Aron Ain of Kronos, the human capital management software company (which incidentally develops technology to record and manage time-keeping) set up in India he told me that this was a top priority. There is more than a working day's time difference – 9.5 hours – between, say, Washington DC and New Delhi. So when the east coast of North America is waking up and going to work, wanting to call co-workers, there's a problem: they are going to bed. This is where technology can of course help. You can join shared platforms and communicate in jet-lag time, not real time. You can observe the etiquette of notifying people when you require them to be 'present'. Aron Ain regularly travels to India to meet employees in person. He says: 'I visit Kronos offices around the world, and the first thing I do is go and say hello to everyone in the office. In India, where there's about 1,000 employees, it takes me a whole morning to go shake hands and say hello.'[12]

It isn't surprising that we love the idea of time travel because it would make our lives so much easier. The Italian theoretical physicist Carlo Rovelli writes wonderfully about time and how in some senses it isn't actually real; at least, 'time doesn't exist at an elementary level. It exists for us'. What he means is that the entire way we measure time is basically a construct in our heads. The speed at which things move, and how quickly or slowly we and other creatures recognize this is very different. Most tellingly, Rovelli helps us understand time zones in relation to feelings. He told *The Guardian* that:

> ... there is a thick emotional layer, which is what gives us the sense of
> the 'flow' of time. The problem of understanding time is the problem
> of disentangling this complex tangle of structures and effects.

Now, it's a big ask to have everyone throw the basic concept of time, time-keeping, time management out of the window, but the philosophy of this is compelling. It does connect to the Simplicity Principle idea of learning from nature. If we recognize – over time of course – that everything we think about time is not exactly wrong but not the whole picture, then maybe this can give us hope that humans can change and help each other do things better and differently once we change our perspective. Just as we are now understanding the climate and nature in a far more intimate way than we did before, such as recognizing that bee survival matters for human survival, there is still time to do something about how we spend and value time itself.

Interruption

The shallow and the deep

But back to the real world of here and now. The world in which we spend around one-third of our lives working (around 10,000 days of our lives) is changing in superfast time. We know that we face huge disruption from the world of work itself – the AI, the shift to free-lance, the shift from full-time office blocks to remote working and co-working spaces for instance – but perhaps the biggest challenge of all is a very human one: Concentration. Remember the question of attention back in the first side of simplicity, Clarity? Remember how fragile it is, how it takes us a third of an hour to regain concentration once we go online and come back off it? Well, interruption is bad and it isn't just about sleep cycles, although I'll come on to body clocks shortly. It is perhaps the biggest waste of time at work any of us face.

I love Cal Newport's work and his definition of 'deep work' which is work requiring undivided attention and deep concentra-tion. In his great book *Deep Work* he writes: 'To simply wait and be bored has become a novel experience in modern life, but from the perspective of concentration training, it's incredibly valuable.'[13] Shallow work is what the digital world creates a lot of. It is the kind that allows us to think we are multitaskers when the human is a natural monotasker. It is when we imagine we are doing simple things but are making our workload and our mental load a lot more complicated. Deep work, on the other hand, is when we turn off our notifications, we shut the door to our office, we put on our headphones, we clear our diary and we focus.

Flexibilism

The days of formally working fixed hours in a fixed place may be numbered. Many of the biggest corporations in the world already have smaller units working out of flexible co-working space (before its fall from grace in the markets in 2019 due to wild over-valuation,

WeWork became one of the largest office tenants in the world with over 11 million square feet of office accommodation) because they understand the 'Teal Organization' mindset that small is better than big.[14] But they also understand that somehow asking people to work in open-plan offices, which became the fashion in office design for several decades, doesn't really work for people. I think we all need 'flexibilism', which is to be flexible about where we work, for how long we work, and how we work.

Some of us like to be in an open-plan atmosphere and it can be good for business. Creativity, brainstorming, and the social sharing can all be vital. In his book about how to love work, Bruce Daisley writes about headphones being 'essentially a coping mechanism: they help their wearers avoid distraction where otherwise they'd be constantly interrupted'.[15] He is right that for some people, some of the time, it's good for concentration and also a good and simple way to signal 'don't come near me, I'm doing deep work'. The British adman Rory Sutherland, who has pioneered applying behavioural change science to advertising, is very clear that the way we work in the office should be *only* social. He argues that it is pointless to imagine we will be able to concentrate when surrounded by others, when it is natural and good to gossip and catch up, and equally pointless to spend hours on a commute if all you do when you arrive is go on email. Incidentally, Rory believes that the next big digital change at work will be a revolution in the way email operates. He thinks that when we get that incoming ping it won't mean it should be answered immediately or even that when we write an email it will be sent immediately, but queued in a more efficient, time-sensitive and imaginative way. I entirely agree.

Body clock

Being sensitive to time is exactly what humans are. I once spent almost all of a business call with the director of a multimillion-dollar global business discussing how we manage jet lag. (Tip: for me it's nothing to eat, drink plenty before the flight but less during, eye masks and melatonin on arrival.) The organizations which do well across different time zones recognize that the practical impact of time and time travel do matter. The idea of staggering on and off the red-eye, then being a good parent or spouse, while coping with altered time zones is not a good recipe for productivity. These organizations have to create different time zones which reflect body and mind clocks too.

We now know a lot more about circadian rhythm – taken from the Latin *circa* (around) and *dies* (day) and also known as the body clock – than we used to. Our internal clocks reflect the earth's rotation around the sun over 24 hours. All our metabolism, hormones and key functions fluctuate in peaks and troughs and are not a one-size-fits-all, nor are they are one-time-fits-all either. For instance, the award-winning neuroscientist Sarah Jayne Blakemore uncovered how teenagers' brains are altered during puberty, making most of the school structure they are forced to operate in wildly unproductive,[16] while recent research from the University of Vigo in Spain has shown that taking blood-pressure medication at night can be more effective than taking it in the morning.

What I read into all of this emerging evidence about chronobiology and the study of our bodies in relation to time inside us, is that we need to radically adjust the way we manage our time outside of our bodies. You could say that this is an example of where we need to avoid being simplistic in order to reach simple solutions. It is becoming obvious that to say that everyone needs to get up at the same time, go to work at the same time, and eat, drink and sleep in the same rythmn is a simplistic solution society has created. It overlooks what is real, which is, well, complicated. So how does the Simplicity Principle apply to this really challenging question of time? Well, start with KISS and Keep It Simple. If you realize you are more productive at one time of the day over another, work with that to the best of your ability. If this means changing policy so that teenagers can concentrate better, why not? That may be complex in the short term, but remember that short term doesn't count in my book as much as the long term does. The long-term solution should be based on simplicity.

All of the shifts to work, the workplace, the working time zones and the working week are here to stay. The more we know about how humans operate, the more we can both adapt machines to help us – like programmes to help workers communicate across different time zones by logging on and off at times to suit – and the more we can change our behaviours to suit the new realities. In addition to keeping it simple, the Simplicity Principle wants to learn from nature. So let's learn: the answer to our productivity crisis and stress crisis may be partly solved, simply, by looking at time and body clocks. Our internal time schedule matters as much as anything on the outside.

Past and present

The past is different from the future. Forwards makes sense, backwards doesn't make sense.[17]

CARLO ROVELLI

We know there is no time like the present. *Carpe diem* is a wonderful Latin phrase which means 'seize the day'. It's a Simplicity Principle kind of a phrase. Like Nike's 'Just Do It'. It makes sense. It cuts down complexity. But letting go of the past can be hard, especially if you live and work in it. So much of how we live is still governed by the past.

We still live and work by an eight-hour office-based day, even though for most of us, our time and our lives is on a never-ending digital loop, where we can live and work in very different ways. The academic Judy Wajcman puts it well when she describes in her book *Pressed for Time* that the smartphone has become 'the quintessential time–space compression mechanism'. She points out that digital devices save time but also consume it.[18] When you think that the average internet user is on it for six hours a day, she's not wrong. So, to be fully in the present, or to imagine the future (which is what humans are really good at doing – imagining) we need to let go of the past. Or at least imagine it doesn't have to be copied. I contributed to a book of essays about how to transform life at work called *Being Present*. One of the essays is by the German generations expert Steffi Burkhart who writes:

> In the past the availability of capital, technology and resources such as oil and gas were the most important drivers for growth, but next to information, data and knowledge gained in real time, human resources will be the scarcest resource of the future.[19]

What she refers to is human capital, human resource, or what we now call Talent.

The simple truth, sweetie, is that talent matters because it is human. You can forget about the machine if you overlook the human. We have to look at ourselves now, as we are, and apply the Simplicity Principle to our lives. This means making decisions now. This means embracing neurodiversity now. This means letting go of old ideas about productivity being about clocking on and off and more about creativity and the ability to be curious. It's about how we rest and reset, and it is about how we learn and understand our limits. How we curb infobesity. How we build relationships with each other. The past can teach us plenty, but we can only react to now. Do the waggle dance like the bee. Tell each other where the pollen is – and where it isn't. Not where it was, that was yesterday. But what's happening right now.

My late brother Joss, the one who told me to 'keep breathing deeply', is with me even though I completed this book five years after he passed away from lung cancer. He stays inside my heart, and so he is present. When he was alive he ran a theatre company which brought back plays from across history into a contemporary setting. He called his theatre company 'Present Moment'. That's a simple instruction: live for today and you want to live tomorrow. But live in the here and now.

SIX FIX

TIME

1 **Don't do deadlines.** Unless you set them yourself. Always question deadline and timeline. Is it real? Should it be done? Or is there another way?

2 **Keep control of your calendar.** Time is a precious resource and needs to be actively managed. Controlling (as far as you can) how you spend it will lead to higher productivity.

3 **Sweeten the gig.** Prepare for freelance life even if it's not happening (yet) and make whatever you do work as far and as flexibly as possible in the time available.

4 **Obey your body clock.** Understand what your body is telling you about how you spend your time. Don't be afraid to look inside before you look outside.

5 **Offices are for water coolers.** Don't bother with an office unless you have to. Work where you need to work if it is internet-related but have a social scene with your colleagues, often.

6 **Live in the present moment.** Focus on what your life and needs are now, and let that be your spur to action, not what has happened in the past.

PART THREE

Hexagon Action in action

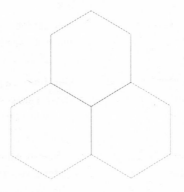

10

Six Hexagon Thinkers

I hope by now you have got the hang of Hexagon Action, in principle at least. I want to show you the achievements of six individuals who for me embody the six ways to achieve focus and productivity of Hexagon Action. I'm therefore calling them Hexagon Thinkers.

Let me recap for those of you who might be flipping straight here without having read earlier sections, that the Simplicity Principle is all about keeping things as lean and simple and focused as possible, thereby cutting through complexity, and that it hinges on looking to find the patterns.

From a chef to a climate change campaigner, these Hexagon Thinkers also live some or all of the six sides you saw in Part Two of this book: Clarity, Individuality, the ability to Reset, and a handle on Knowledge, Networks and Time – all of which they address in ways which cut through complexity and achieve a simplicity which is focused and productive. They will, I hope, set you doing your own thinking. Let me introduce them to you now:

1 Massimo Bottura

2 Faith Osier

3 Satish Kumar

4 Arianna Huffington

5 Jessica Morris

6 Greta Thunberg

Massimo Bottura

Massimo Bottura is an Italian chef. Not just any Italian chef. His restaurant, Osteria Francescana, tucked away in the Emilia-Romagna region (famous for *parmigiano reggiano* cheese, *prosciutto di Parma* and the best balsamic vinegar), is consistently listed as one of the top restaurants in the world. He is now one of a handful – probably a hexagon handful at that – of top global chefs who everybody in the haute cuisine world has heard of and, frankly, worships. Coincidentally his breakthrough started with a six-themed dish called 'Six Tortellini Walking into a Broth', which was a beautiful example of the geometry and power of design and craft.

Massimo is as much an artist as he is a chef. His mission was always to transform the Italian kitchen basics of 'grandmother' cooking – home-made pasta specifically – into a modern take. There was just one problem: in Italy in the 1980s and 1990s, when he began, he faced huge resistance from his Italian customers who wanted lasagne the old-fashioned way. At the beginning he had no customers. They boycotted his restaurant. He says there was a moment when he realized he had to embrace his creative individuality even if it meant scandalizing everyone in the process, and that the best way to scandalize and stick to his guns was to produce a timeless Italian dish in a very novel and individual way. Thus 'Six Tortellini Walking into a Broth' turned on its head the idea of a big bowl of steaming home-made pasta parcels filled with meat, and instead placed six tiny tortellini on a board, marching in a straight line towards, well, a bowl of broth.

The effect of this was to do a couple of things. Firstly, it signalled that Massimo was not on the run from his critics. In fact, they flocked to him after that. But it also did create a new genre: a highly original take on classic dishes. For instance, lasagne became 'The crunchy part of the lasagne' featuring a giant crisped pasta resembling what the chef says 'is the best part of the lasagne, always, from childhood: you want the crunchy burnt corner'. Finally, after several years, during which everyone caught up with his genius, and thanks to a great review (restaurant reputations are made or broken by the right review at the right time) this approach began to work with local and regional customers and then internationally. Osteria Francescana has three Michelin stars and in 2018 took the top spot in the World's 50 Best Restaurants list. Massimo Bottura put originality at the heart of his restaurant's food using the best ingredients from nature, and it all works: deliciously. Which hexagon object most brings Massimo Bottura to mind for me? Probably the quilt, with its creativity, originality, community aspect and its gentleness.

Faith Osier

Faith Osier is the first African and the second woman to be elected president of the International Union of Immunological Societies (IUIS). She is a multi-award-winning Kenyan scientist, mother and Professor of Malaria Immunity at Oxford University. She studies how humans acquire immunity to malaria in order to develop a new, more effective vaccine, in the hope of eradicating this age-old and devastating disease once and for all. She says she 'loves to simplify science and communicate it to diverse audiences'. She is a TED Fellow and her talk *The Key to a Better Malaria Vaccine* has had over 1.5 million views.[1]

Faith's focus on simplicity is one reason she is a Hexagon Thinker. In her TED talk, she argues that while technology from 'advanced imaging and omics platforms... have given us a clearer view of just how complex the parasite really is', the prevailing approach to vaccine design has remained rudimentary. In order to make a more effective vaccine, we must go back to basics. We need to look to nature and understand how our bodies deal with this complexity. As she argues, we need to combine 'cutting-edge technology with century-old insights'. Her team sought to understand how people who are frequently infected with malaria acquire immunity. Their research sought to build on and improve on what had been learned this far (one of our knowledge axioms); it smethod was to 'collapse 30 years of research into one three-month-long experiment'. It was driven by the simple question 'What does a successful antibody response look like?' Her team identified over 200 proteins many of which were not on the radar for malaria vaccines and which they believe 'could provide the breakthroughs that we need to make malaria history through vaccination'.

A strong sense of Purpose drives her, as she reminds us that eradicating malaria 'would save half a million lives every year. Two hundred million cases. It's estimated that malaria costs Africa $12 billion a year. So this is economics. Africa would simply thrive.'

Faith also champions diversity and is a leader that seeks to bring others with her: another reason that she embodies Hexagon Action. She is passionate about inspiring and building the capacity of African men and women, to be 'engaged internationally in science and leadership' and 'deliver the interventions needed on the continent'. She also champions smart collaboration and the sharing of ideas: indeed she leads SMART – the South-South Malaria Antigen Research Partnership, a 'network of African scientists which puts collaboration at its centre to share resources and collective expertise to accelerate the search for highly effective malaria vaccines'.

The hexagon-shaped object which Faith Osier brings to mind is the dragonfly eye: each compound eye on the dragonfly is hexagonal, containing up to 30,000 hexagonal facets that go practically all round its head, allowing an incredibly broad field of vision round, above and below. The all-seeing and all-seeking scientist needs a dragonfly attitude and eye like Faith Osier!

Satish Kumar

'When you think you need to press the button, stop for a minute and have a fresh cup of tea.' This statement does not seem terribly radical, talking about buttons and cups of tea, except that when you think that 'the button' meant nuclear weapons, and that the person meant offering a simple cup of tea as the best action between war and peace, it takes on a different meaning.

The phrase was uttered to leaders in New Delhi, Moscow, Paris, London and Washington DC during a historic 'Peace Walk' made by the Indian peace campaigner Satish Kumar during the 1970s. He was an outlier for the kind of activism we see today around the environment: being entirely simple and straightforward in the message, and operating with complete integrity. Satish Kumar was born in Rajasthan in India and when he was just 9 years old he left his family to become a Jain monk, advocating a life of simplicity. By the time I met him, he was a world-famous figure in his seventies living in the UK, and was just as humble, just as spiritual. In a hill-top retreat, in front of a small audience I had convened, he recounted his famous Peace Walk. Despite his humble origins and the lack of technology or the kind of easy travel offered today to more or less everyone, the young Satish Kumar was inspired to change the world, and to do that he resolved to go around the world, on foot, preaching peace. Together with a friend, the 20-something Satish embarked on an 8,000-mile peace pilgrimage with no money and depending only the kindness and hospitality of strangers.

Can you imagine walking further than the station? Well, they walked from India to the United States, via Moscow, London and Paris, to deliver a humble packet of 'peace tea' to the then leaders of the world's four nuclear powers of the time. 'I got through eight pairs of shoes, lots of blisters, knee pain, going up to 10–11,000 feet of high mountains, then down, then up: lots of pain. And hunger,' he said in an interview.[2]

When he was in his fifties he undertook a 2,000-mile walk around Britain to all the holy places he could reach to celebrate love and nature. It is obvious why I describe Satish as a Hexagon Thinker: he champions simplicity and a connection to nature. On simplicity itself one of his recent books is called *Elegant Simplicity*. He wrote:

> When my friend Menon and I crossed the border from India to Pakistan during our Peace Walk, I said, 'If we go as Indians, we will meet Pakistanis, Russians, or Americans. If we go as Hindus, we will meet Muslims, Christians, Buddhists, or Jews. If we go as Gandhians, we'll meet capitalists, communists, or socialists. These are all labels which divide us. I don't want to go as an Indian, a Hindu, a Gandhian. I want to go simply as a human being; then wherever I go I will meet human beings. I'll be able to make friends with all of them.'

On nature, Satish is equally eloquent, saying: 'We are part of one Earth community. Trees are our kith and kin, birds flying in the sky, bees and wasps, butterflies and snakes, tigers and elephants are all our kith and kin.'

Satish Kumar's hexagonal mascot has to be the lava columns, huge magisterial basalt hexagons which form throughout the world from Japan to Ireland, the result of hot lava cooling down.[3] Satish's missions to cool and calm wise heads the world over makes this the right metaphor for his particular form of Hexagon Action.

Arianna Huffington

I first met Arianna Huffington in New York after my book *Fully Connected* about Social Health in an age of overload was published and we instantly hit it off. I was with my teenage daughter and noticed that Arianna paid her a good deal of interest and attention, which was a generous thing to do. We talked fairly nonstop about ideas about wellbeing and she asked if I would become editor-at-large for her new wellbeing and productivity platform, Thrive Global. I instantly agreed. My daughter is rather hard to impress but told me afterwards in that condescending teenage way, 'I thought that was a good meeting, mum.'

Anyone who meets Arianna Huffington remembers doing so. She is a forceful character and uses her charm and influence to move the needle on some very tough issues. Arianna is a polymath, someone who uses their wide knowledge and interest. Really, she is a human honey bee: incredibly hard-working, very involved on the ground in what she produces, building up a team. She is not a cocooned and protected queen bee but the architect of a social community. She loves the buzz of connecting different people and ideas, of cross-pollinating from politics to business to health. In her career this charismatic Greek-American, Cambridge-educated feminist has championed spiritualism, environmentalism and art. She regularly appears on the world's 'Top' lists such as *Time*'s 100 Most Influential People and *Forbes*' Most Powerful Women.

Having set up the hugely successful *Huffington Post* blogging platform she turned to wellbeing, health and productivity with Thrive Global, and began to write international bestsellers on subjects which had until that point languished in special interest areas of bookshops. Her book *Thrive* was the first major book to put the whole issue of 'always on' and digital overload on to the map, and began to give all of us permission to think about our lives a little differently. She followed this up with *The Sleep Revolution* which triggered a huge ongoing movement, new research and a global awareness that sleep is the baseline for all physical and mental health.[4] All the aspects of the six sides of simplicity – Clarity, Individuality, Reset, Knowledge, Networks and Time – are ones which she addresses in her work, and the six Hexagon Action priorities of achieving simple cut-through, connecting to our natural selves and the spiritual world, through to the versatile but brilliantly formatted geometry of her websites are all in sync with Hexagon Action itself. What would her hexagon mascot be? The hive of course. The ultimate hexagon is the hive, which is painstak-ingly put together, and in which all the magic and mystery of the honey bee ecosystem resides.

Jessica Morris

Jessica Morris is a British woman in her fifties who worked in communications and brought up her family before one day, out hiking, out of the blue, she collapsed. She was diagnosed with brain cancer of the most deadly kind: glioblastoma, or GBM. For her family and large circle of friends like me, this was devastating. But within weeks of surgery Jessica was back on fighting form, declar-ing that she would dedicate her life to 'turning glioblastoma from terminal to treatable' and setting up the first GBM patient-data-gathering app for patients and a non-profit called OurBrainBank.[5] She started a blog. She started a Facebook group. OurBrainBank began to campaign not just for funding but for policy changes at the highest level.

The whole point of OurBrainBank is Social Health – function-ing connections in a digital age. Specifically, it is about making sure that Knowledge, Networks and Time are harnessed well together. Jessica realized that not only was some knowledge about clinical trials and treatments not getting to patients, but that the vital infor-mation from their changing daily symptoms and treatment responses were not being communicated effectively to their doctors. This is also against a background of overwhelming infobesity about the clinical condition itself. So the OurBrainBank network has been used to clarify, streamline and convey information in a useful way between patients, their carers and doctors. And time: most GBM patients are very short of it, and Jessica writes and broadcasts often about how little time many patients may have. But she uses this fact to propel her efforts and everyone around her into action. She has a natural flair for communicating and campaigning, and a keen awareness that the science of brain cancer is changing every day.

I would say that Jessica is the ultimate non-profit campaigner, the hero of every non-profit in every city in every country. She is both queen bee and worker bee: everyone fights hard for her because she is so unique. Yet she rolls up her sleeve, often within days of surgery, and comes roaring back. She wants to change the climate on cancer. Not just her kind of cancer, but all cancers. She thinks laterally and very precisely about how to do that: there is geometry, pattern, focus, productivity in everything she does. But also creativity and curiosity. She wants to know everything she can, to share it and empower her community. What is her hexagon mascot? It has to be the molecular structure of carbon, which, while not a hexagon shape itself, forms into almost indestructible carbon complex forms such as graphite and the diamond, and without which most organic life – including humans – would be lost.

Greta Thunberg

One of the great news images of recent years is of a young Swedish school girl with pigtails sitting on a pavement with a placard behind her which reads 'Skolstrejk föor Klimatet' which translates as 'School Strike for the Climate'. This picture became a gamechanger in the profile of climate change, and turbocharged world leaders, the world's media and the world's young people and climate change campaigners. It is the deep connection to nature and the inspiration to protect it which immediately makes Greta Thunberg a Hexagon Thinker.

Then there is the simplicity of her argument and how it cuts through the usual thicket of argument you normally get in politics. As she wrote in a Facebook post:

Yes, the climate crisis is the most complex issue we have ever faced. But the solution is black and white; we need to stop the emissions of greenhouse gases. There are no grey areas when it comes to survival.

So, the first reason is the environment and her commitment to nature, and the second is her clarity, her decisiveness, and the simplicity of her argument. The third is her neurodiversity, part of the Simplicity Six axiom on Individuality. She is the first global figure to be neurodiverse and to put her difference centre-stage. Indeed, in the same Facebook post she wrote about her Asperger's diagnosis as 'a gift' and said:

> If I would have been 'normal' and social I would have organized myself in an organization, or started an organization by myself. But since I am not that good at socializing I did this instead.

In today's infobese world, where the cut-through is usually loud and ugly, Greta Thunberg represents something else: individuality, authenticity, and fearlessness. She has cut through, as she said: 'I only speak when I think it's necessary. Now is one of those moments. A whisper is sometimes louder than shouting.'

Greta Thunberg, who was named *Time* Magazine's Person of the Year 2019, did not ask to become a global heroine to some, nor did she ask to become the object of derision and hate which has also happened.[6] Rather like a hexagonal shape itself, she has proved to be tremendously strong and resistant: remember how graphite is one hundred times stronger than steel. 'The Greta Effect' has been named after her, and the strength of her influence. For instance, Swedish rail declared an 8 per cent rise in rail travel due to concerns about CO_2 emissions from flying, with a new hashtag #istayonthe-ground developing to deter air travel.[7] If bees could campaign, wouldn't they do so against pesticides? They perhaps need their own Greta. I think the hexagon mascot representing her has to be the snowflake: highly sensitive, individual, and very unique.

11

Be the bee

Role and responsibility in a complex world

Where the bee sucks, there suck I,
In a cowslip's bell I lie,
There I couch when owls do cry,
On the bat's back I do fly
After summer merrily.
   Merrily, merrily shall I live now
   Under the blossom that lies on the bough.

ARIEL IN *THE TEMPEST*

When I started to research this book, I spent a lot of time at our cottage in the middle of the Brecon Beacons in the middle of Wales, where honey bees literally drank from honeysuckle and wild lavender right outsight my window, beyond which plump Welsh cattle and sheep grazed. I went into the local town, Hay-on-Wye, home to the biggest collection of second-hand bookstores in the world and the famous book festival visited several times by my great mentor–friend Maya Angelou, and I stumbled across a treasure-trove of old books about bees. I confess I was less interested in how bees make honey and so avoided books about how to become a beekeeper. Instead, I wanted to know how bees behave, how they actually live, what roles they play? I came across a real beauty of book, written in 1939 called *The Mind of the Bees* and written by Julien Françon, about whom I can find nothing except this fine book. Here he is on what happens when bees go foraging:

> As soon as the sun has topped the crest of the hill, if the weather be not threatening, for they fear cold and storm, they hurl themselves from the hive with attending flight which leads them towards the flowers, the purveyors of nectar and pollen which it is their mission to collect.[1]

Many of us recognize that feeling. Hurling ourselves from home or the office, launching into a mission either domestic or professional, almost on automatic pilot. Who we are in the world and what we do in it defines us. Bees, like us, have a fairly recognizable set of things they do on an hourly, daily, ongoing basis. Let me focus on just six of their core functions:

1 They create and nurture life.

2 Bees build and repair where they live and work.

3 Bees collect goods with which to make and store products.

4 Bees allow other living creatures to flourish (cross-pollination).

5 They work incredibly hard and efficiently but they also rest and replenish.

6 And finally, because they are a social species too, they communicate, albeit wordlessly.

Foraging, dancing and pollinating

Role play

Every bee, despite only having a finite set of functions and skills, is probably more individual than we think. Certainly, there are 20,000 separate species of Apis alone, but as research of other social insects such as termites is uncovering, they may even have actual personality traits we are only just beginning to uncover.[2] (Termites, it turns out, are not universally industrious: some under infrared scrutiny are what can politely be called slackers, while others are workaholic. Sound familiar in your life?)

But for all of their individuality, bees, and the honey bees we are focusing on in Hexagon Action do have fixed roles. There is only one queen, tens of thousands of female worker bees, and smaller numbers of male drones. They all have specific tasks which only they do. The queen lays eggs, for instance, and the workers perform a variety of tasks from keeping brood cells warm in the hexagonal hives to going out to forage in the field and coming back in to do the waggle dance. Yes, the waggle dance is an important role for a bee to play. It is when it conveys all the information it has picked up in its antennae to the other bees to tell them how far the nearest store of pollen is and where exactly it is located.

When I coach people in career transition I often ask them to identify very specific roles they could play in their next phase of life. Often they look blank, or scared. I try and tell them that the structure of identifying what they can do is actually helpful. Sometimes looking at the bee is a good way to get them to focus and put their own skills into focus:

1 **Waggler:** The waggle is a very good skill to have. I think I have it in life (although ironically I am a terrible dancer). But if someone is a good communicator it could mean they have skills in anything from writing speeches to internal communications. Or it could mean they have good people skills overall. If you can be trusted and listened to, you can convey and store vital information which is valuable for all.

2 **Queen (or Leader):** We think we know a lot about the queen bee, but interestingly the cultural association with that term is negative: To be a 'queen bee' is to be aloof, grand, not with the

gang, and yet to have power. Translate this into leadership: are you the kind of leader who connects with your team? Inspiring loyalty if you lead is not easy to achieve and comes because you are regarded with respect and because you are seen to be essential to the survival of the group.

3 **Forager:** These bees go out and search for the honey; they remind me of people in sales and development or recruitment, who must to go out and find out things and find out people. Are you a forager or do others need to play that role in your life? This is an especially valuable question to ask if you are a freelance person, or developing a portfolio career. Many of the people I coach and teach are being forced by working practices to become foragers – and they don't feel at all comfortable doing it. People learn, like bees, to forage.

4 **Pollinators:** Bees create most of our feed through pollinating millions of flowers and crops. Without them, humans would struggle to survive. In human terms, those who can cross-pollinate ideas, be flexible, partake in what is called in network theory 'boundary spanning' are all highly valuable members of society. They don't consume so much as spread, collect, and mix it up.

5 **Worker bees:** The main worker is the essential driver of delivery. The worker bees create the honeycomb from wax that they produce from their bodies. They gather all of the nectar used to make honey. There is absolutely nothing wrong with just being able to work hard. To do what is asked of you without complaint. In fact, this is often overlooked. But the worker bee is literally the centre of production. Which means, yes, the hive of productivity. If you can be clear how you contribute, what your role is in the creation of the product of whatever organization you belong to, that is value. Pure and simple.

6 **Housekeeper:** Bees are especially good at housekeeping, which is one reason why they are so productive: nothing is wasted, much is recycled. Workers care for the eggs and the larvae, raise

the young bees, clean the nest, get rid of dead bees and other debris, defend the nest, and feed the queen. Your role could quite literally be to be in charge of the house – that's what a 'chief of staff' does, which is a grand way of saying: supervise.

There is obviously a huge difference between us humans and our tiny, stripy, honey-loving fellow social creatures. I would not want you to take 'be the bee, honey' too literally. But the way they organize themselves in different roles, and their social essence means that if we want to really apply the Simplicity Principle, and learn to *keep it simple* and *learn from nature*, then they are the living species we can look to and learn from.

I hope this chapter and all you have read so far allows you to go out foraging for a new and improved way of living. All that is left is to recap what I've covered out there in the forest of words I have created to share with you. See where you land with it.

12

Six-Fixes + 6

Practice, they say, makes perfect. And the best thing about the number six, other than it being the number of sides on a hexagon, is that it is mathematically 'perfect'. So practise your Hexagon Action and you'll figure out what works perfectly for you while you put the Simplicity Principle to the test: your own life.

This chapter offers some very action-orientated ideas. After all, it's all about what you do, not what you say. First, here is a recap on the six sides of simplicity and their Six-Fixes.

1 Clarity

The axiom of Clarity is that 'Being crystal-clear brings you simplicity.' There is nothing worse than muddle, confusion, which brings with it delay, miscommunication, distrust. When you are clear about something others get Clarity. So being clear is an act of generosity. Not being clear often has a knock-on effect. It affects, for instance, your networks. It badly affects knowledge and information flows. The six core ingredients of Clarity are *Decision, Attention, Purpose, Habit, Boundaries* and what I call *Housekeeping*. The hexagonal shape which speaks most to Clarity for me is the Lonsdaleite diamond, which, thanks to its hexagonal lattice and its amorphous carbon composition, makes it one of the hardest structures on earth.[1]

Clarity Six-Fix

i   **Prevent decision fatigue.** Keep your decisions down, make them by using Hexagon Action to really home in on your choices.

ii **Pay attention to attention!** The more you scroll, the more you lose those 23 minutes and 15 seconds getting your attention back. Avoid the infinite scroll.

iii **Take a Techno-Shabbat.** Find a time when you get physical not digital, and make that day or even part of a day your 'Techno-Shabbat'. Look at all your rituals and embrace habit, even if you start one to break another.

iv **Puzzle your Productivity.** Are you being productive? If not, why not? Could Purpose be the key?

v   **Just Say No.** Choose what you say yes to and don't be afraid to say no. Boundaries are good!

vi **Cultivate a tidy mind.** De-clutter surrounding, even if that means rearranging the mess you like: **but** be clear what your process is to find something when you need it.

2 Individuality

The six-word axiom of Individuality is that **'Humans should take priority over machines.'** We have to work extra-hard in a digital age to know where the human stops and the machine starts, and this brings tremendous anxiety and confusion as well as opportunity. The six-sided elements which help us stay stable and solid in difficult, shifting times are *Identity, The Digital Self, Neurodiversity, Creativity, Integrity* and a keen sense of *Place*. The hexagonal mascot for this side of the hexagon of simplicity is, of course, the snowflake: literally no two snowflakes are ever the same.

Individuality Six-Fix

i   Be the Snowflake. Reclaim the idea of being a 'Snowflake' and think of sensitivity/neurodiversity not as a negative, politically motivated concept but as one based on reality, compassion and embracing difference.

ii   Be your true creative self. Remember that who you are online is not the same person exactly, and that the real you is the one to stay connected with above all others. And notice your creativity even in the ordinary everyday.

iii   Be wary of groupthink. We all want to belong but to follow what everyone else is doing with blind faith leads to a closed not an open mindset. You can hold a different view to the others, you know.

iv   Be the Chief Happiness Officer. Ask if you can be the person who inspires and champions wellbeing because you embody it yourself. Use creativity to guide wellbeing.

v   Have integrity. Often we are afraid to be individual and to raise our heads above the parapet. The result? We draw ourselves into a tangled web of complication. Remember the three 3C: Calling It Out, Compassion, Compromise. This is about being practical and centred in what is real: it's not so much 'No' as 'Let's do it like this instead'.

vi   Know your Place. The honey bee always goes home or builds a new home. The sense of place for bees, both in terms of where they live and also where they go out to, is incredibly strong...

Where we live, where we work, the distance we travel between the two: the simplicity of the journey and the arrangement matters a great deal.

3 Reset

What six-word axiom best sums up this vital life recipe? **'The always-on mind needs rest.'** We know a lot about sleep these days, but rest and resetting is not quite the same thing. Part of the epidemic of stress which is sweeping around the world is directly thanks to the 'always-on' culture. The six workarounds I have chosen to highlight are *Release, Mind-less-ness, Curiosity, Nature, Breath* and *Fun.* What hexagonal shape most conjures up Reset? Well, for me it has to be the quilt, that beautiful arts and craft activity which puts the hexagonal shape at the very centre of its pattern for so much of the time.

Reset Six-Fix

i   **Set to zero.** Sleep is vital but so is a wider sense of Reset. How you recharge when you are awake or during waking hours is in your hands. Identify what works for you in order to set your tension levels back to zero.

ii   **Mind-less-ness.** Find your way to achieve serenity, switch off and be still – literally or figuratively. Meditation may be your way but it doesn't have to be what anyone else does. Discover what helps you switch off or what excites and stimulates your creative juices.

iii   **Active rest.** Seek out a change in scenery and let your Curiosity fuel ideas, inspiration, energy. Notice what is happening, and be a tourist wherever you are. Return with renewed focus.

iv **Be where the bees and trees are!** Reconnect with the rhythm and pace of nature – the great re-balancer – and notice the contrast when you emerge.

v **Take a breath and a breather.** Sometimes we need a quick Reset, not to switch off entirely. When things get intense, cultivate techniques to calm yourself by focusing on breath, or take a breather – a moment to individually or collectively readjust.

vi **Find a football.** Find the activity which you can do which is unquestionably fun. If you aren't smiling or laughing in your day, you aren't having enough of it!

4 Knowledge

The six-word rule here is that **'Escaping from infobesity must come first.'** I call how we manage our connections and connectedness in the digital age Social Health. Just like we have learned to manage physical and mental health through diet and exercise, we must now understand that we are in the middle of a digital infobesity epidemic and this brings a whole range of Social Health problems. The six recipes for overcoming infobesity are *Trust, Wisdom, Known Unknowns, Learn, Curate* and *Remember.* Which hexagon best conveys this axiom? It has to be Saturn's Hexagon, the extraordinary, and largely unexplained cloud pattern which surrounds the planet Saturn, which lies sixth from the sun.

Knowledge Six-Fix

i **Prioritize trust.** To decipher fact from fiction, try and keep it simple. Start by asking whether there is more to it than meets the eye. Are you being wilfully blind because you want to believe it? Step back: can you trace the source of the knowledge and can you trust it?

ii **Use your antennae.** Wisdom combines experience, feeling and knowledge. Be the bee in this: use your antennae. Use your sixth sense. Bring this to the table, either the boardroom table or the coffee counter or the meeting room: bring what you *know already.*

iii **Look for Known Unknowns.** Imagine and anticipate the Known Unknowns if you can. Accept that there are Known Unknowns… but don't be caught out by ignoring the possibility of one you might be able to do something about after all.

iv **Join the soft skills revolution.** Brush up on your hard skills and technical skills but don't neglect the soft ones. Can you negotiate well, hold a conversation well, show your empathy?

v **Use a Knowledge Dashboard.** Cut through the fatty tissue of TMI (too much information) – while also providing variety and diversity, crucial ingredients for Social Health as with physical health.

vi **Remember the perfect number.** There is only so much anyone can remember, so bear in mind the limits of the working memory.

5 Networks

The axiom for this vital recipe is stark: **'Diverse networks matter more than networking.'** There is a huge amount to know about how to gain simplicity by focusing on this area alone, because networks underpin everything in nature and in technology. The more we understand, the better we can practise creating rich networks of our own. The six-pack here contains the *Hierarchy of Communication, Superorganism, Networks,* and the 'Triple S' of *Social Capital, Salons* and *Social Six.* What have I chosen as the networks hexagon? It has to be the beehive. The bees are the poster-species for simplicity and Hexagon Action. The network of cells inside a hive are always – and I do mean always – made of hexagons. And the hive thrives because of its unique hexagonal cellular system.

Networks Six-Fix

i   Be face-to-face in a Facebook world. The hierarchy of communication keeps us focused on how much time we do and don't spend connecting with people in real life, and of the value of keeping it natural: face-to-face. Be honest: are you hiding behind screen-based network? Though it may be much more time-consuming, this is where the real value lies. It also forces you to prioritize and focus on what matters most.

ii   Think peoplebase not database. Remember that everyone wants to be a name, not a number. Organize who you know and how you communicate based not on quantity, but on quality of relationships.

iii   Networks, not networking. The best way to think about networking is to adopt a relational not transactional mindset; think not *what can I get out of it?* but *how can I forge a connection with someone?* Networks will flow from (smaller) events organized to prioritize people and content.

iv   Be social. Create social capital by being part of communities, because it strengthens them and it strengthens you. Like bees we thrive on shared specialized knowledge and draw on swarm intelligence to make better decisions.

v   Coffee-houses not conferences. Recreate the salon and the coffee-house in small, intimate gatherings, and don't think that a large conference is a good substitute: they are different.

vi   Social Six. Take stock, and identify your 'Social Six'. Who are the six or so people in your networks who really matter to you now, and who you can count on when you need to get things done?

6 Time

However we count and calculate, we cannot stretch time. **'Treat your time like your body'** means that what you put in your schedule is as important as what you eat and drink in terms of your Social Health – the way you manage the connected era. Research shows we spend about six hours a day now online.[2] How do we learn to value time and spend it wisely, to control it and make it work for the Simplicity Principle? The six time-related recipes I focus on are: *Deadline, Schedule, Time Zones, Interruption, Body Clocks,* and *Past and Present*. The hexagon shape for time is the humble soap bubble. The hexagon is loved in physics because it always seeks to be most efficient for space. The hexagonal soap bubble conveys all that is messy about time as well as how much we want to cram, efficiently, into it.

Time Six-Fix

i **Don't do deadlines.** Unless you set them yourself. Always question deadline and timeline: is it real? Should it be done? Or is there another way?

ii **Keep control of your calendar.** Time is a precious resource and needs to be actively managed; controlling (as far as you can) how you spend will lead to higher productivity.

iii **Get in the time zone.** Figure out what your real time zone is: do you need to try and restructure when you are your most productive?

iv **Obey your body clock.** Understand what your body is telling you about how you spend your time. Don't be afraid to look inside before you look outside.

v **Offices are for water coolers.** Don't bother with an office unless you have to. Work where you need to work if it is internet-related but have a social scene with your colleagues, often.

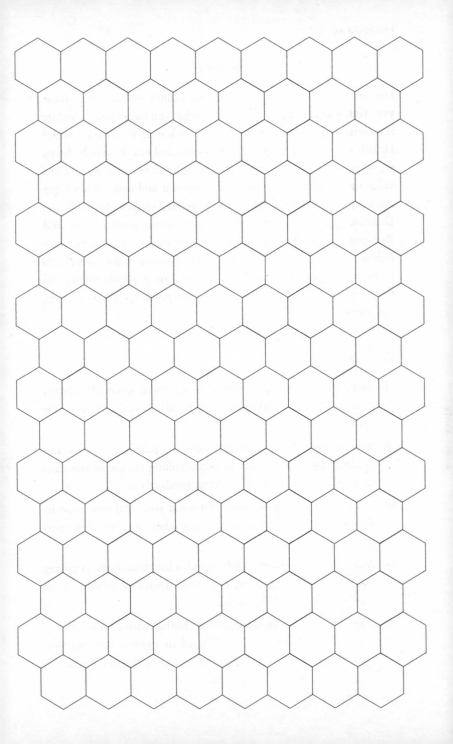

vi Live today as you want to live tomorrow. Don't waste time and use past experience but not as the best measure of what you do now or next. Focus on what your life and needs are now, and put them into action.

Six more ideas

Now for six more ideas to think about. I recommend you invest in some hexagonal paper or notepads, and that you start to play around on the page and online with the shape of the hexagon, to see whether you want to visually think in sides, sixes and connecting patterns or just follow these ideas in a more word-based way.

1 Half a hexagon

They say that a problem shared is a problem halved. How about a hexagon? A hexagon actor shares and cross-pollinates problems as well as doing so with solutions. First, identify three things going on for you right now you want to fix or improve. Use this half-a-hexagon to jot down the overall 'thing'. Keep the top half of the hexagon for problems and the bottom half for possible solutions. Next, think about someone with whom you can share quite a specific problem: someone from your Social Six perhaps. See if they can help you figure out a new angle, or take a different side to the view you are taking.

2 Hexa-mapping

I'm sure you are familiar with mind-mapping, but what about trying it out yourself with some hexagons?

'Hexa' is the Greek for 'six' and hexa-mapping is a way for you to play around with the slides and sides you want to focus on. Hexagon Action is a framework, not a rigid rule. If you have a steady hand you can of course sketch these hexagons. Name each hexagon something you want to focus on and then identify the six edges of it that matter or overlap. The graph paper helps you draw out lines between different issues and it is always interesting to look at how long some lines are compared to others, and how tightly packed other issues are when you take this particular mapping action.

3 Time zones

If you often feel, in the middle of the day, that you can't quite remember what you have done or what you still have left to do (almost like a kind of jet lag), try creating personal Time Zones. This is basically a set of daily boundaries about what you do and when. No one is a functioning machine every second of the day. Most of us are awake for fifteen hours or so. Discount three hours just to *live* – get up, go back down again, get someone else up and off to school: whatever. So that leaves something like twelve hours each day to get things done in, and feel creative, connected and in tune with simplicity. As a framework, loosely divide the day into six sections of two hours each. Then identify six (of course) kinds of activities which are regular for you each day. The trick is to be flexible but also fixed: to bunch and group things to be efficient but to allow space and enough variety to avoid boredom or sitting down in one place too long. Personalize of course, but a general template is:

(i) **Travel** - on foot, on the metro, in a car. Is this thinking time, or listening time, or making calls time, or just being on your feet and moving time?

(ii) **Process** - as in dealing with the Inbox, or preparing the lunchbox. Try and avoid mixing it up by dipping in and out of social stuff. Keep to mono, not multitasking here.

(iii) **People.** Who do you need or want to see, to meet with, to break bread with, to hang out with? Remember the Hierarchy of Communications from the Networks (page 149): don't skimp on meeting people if it is the right thing to do.

(iv)   **Project.** If I don't spend two hours on most days doing something which has a visible end result - from de-cluttering a cuboard to a piece of writing, I feel that jet lag dislocation of time not being mine. Try and complete something which really needs doing each day.

(v)   **Mind-less-ness.** Be in Reset mode, even for 20 minutes, a third of an hour. Or give yourself three such breaks but again, no multi-tasking, that's not resting.

(vi)   Finally, **Physical.** I do mean exercise, I do mean movement. Above all I mean: Not digital. There has to be time set aside for that, each and every day.

4 *Six-lists*

Who doesn't love writing a list? So helpful but only if you limit the 'to do' part and also focus on the 'when to do' part. But a six-list is really about organizing whatever you are doing into a list of six ways you approach anything from an enjoyable task to a problematic one. So here you go:

1   Sit for six minutes with a problem and review before and after.

2   Gather your Social Six around you for a brainstorm or a social event.

3   Think in cycles of six days, six weeks, six months: what do you see? Use a hexa-map to plan that out.

4   Clear out six things in your to-do list. Be like Arianna Huffington and Warren Buffet and reduce complexity!

5   Make your Knowledge Dashboard and start curating your own information sources.

6   Have a Saturn Saturday. Make sure you have a complete day of rest, of Reset and of refocus, once a week.

How are all these hexagons and sixes relevant to you? Here's how. Just like a football is there to be kicked in order to play and hopefully win a game, using hexagons to play around with, whether on paper, in your head, or as an organizing principle, will help you – to use a football analogy – get your goal. If you find this feels complicated or not right, stop. Connect with what you feel, and the simple way will almost certainly come to you if you have patience, focus and give it your full attention.

5 Year-round resolutions

Have you tried a different kind of zone, which is to divide not your day into six kinds of things you need to get done, but your year? I know it's common to begin each January with a long list of New Year's resolutions but these always seem to die like diets before too long. I prefer to keep it simple as you know. I identify six goals at the start of each year. These can be specific ('Learn Spanish' or 'Set a date night each Wednesday') or they can be more broad and general ('Be more generous and compassionate' or 'Keep my individuality and call it out more'). Review them every six weeks or so. Do they feel as relevant? If you aren't keeping to them, maybe you need to focus on just one, or change it up. What matters is owning your intention and reviewing it. Keeping it simple but not necessarily unambitious: think big, as befits life goals!

6 The hexagon and the honey bee

Finally, think of six ways you can slow down, scale down, and connect with what nature teaches us about finding simple solutions. Here's six to get you going:

1 Use pen and paper for six hours (days if you can manage it) instead of writing documents digitally, and always have a notepad and pen.

2 Have a 'face-to-face Friday' instead of a 'dress-down Friday'. A day when you just meet people physically, not virtually.

3 Plant some flowers for a bee. If you don't have a garden, go to a public space where you can be near the bees, and do what you can to help them pollinate their environment – and ours.

4 Go slow. Walk and notice. Do this at least six times a week for as long as you can.

5 Scale back. Do less. Achieve more. Keep it simple.

6 Sit in the sun where possible and just... be.

Think of all of these as a connected set of hexagons which form patterns you notice and know you can change or alter. Nature shows us that nothing is fixed for long. I bought a lovely set of hexagon LED lights which can form all sorts of different shapes on a wall in my kitchen. Sometimes I have them all lit up, firing my enthusiasm and focus. At other times I notice I have kept some of them dark and that the pattern I put them in changes with my mood and the individual demands of the day. Put this book down for 60 seconds every now and then and just think: what is coming *into your head?* For most people, beginning these exercises inevitably feels a bit odd and forced. Persevere a little bit. Practice makes perfect. Just like the number six and just like that perfect hexagonal honeycomb cell. Go on, be the bee. We need you, buzzing away creatively, individually, powerfully. Keep it simple. Learn from nature. Good luck. And thank you for being on this journey with me.

ACKNOWLEDGEMENTS

Thanks to everyone who helped me build this honeycomb of ideas. To the brilliant team at Kogan Page especially Chris Cudmore, Helen Kogan, Jaini Haria, Martin Hill, Susan Hodgson and Amy Joyner; Kim Wylie at Ingram Publishing Services; Marissa Eigenbrood and Mike Onorato at Smith Publicity and Shona Abhyankar at ed public relations. Thanks as ever to my agents Elizabeth Sheinkman at PFD and Eithne Jones at Speaker Ideas. Gratitude to Rachel Horigan for her impeccable late-stage research and fact-checking and to Lesley Levene for her additional editorial eyes. To my wonderful team at Editorial Intelligence including Laura Musins, Sophie Radice, Shanice Shields-Mills, Karen Persad and Hayden Brown. I am lucky to work with such an incredible group of professionals, and each of them very lovely human beings too.

For being supportive, being themselves, and always being there for me – Alaric and our brood: Roman, Anoushka, Wolfgang and their big siblings Rachael and Max. My mum Marlene and brother Andy and our large extended family. And Mitzi, Levi and Dapple: I can't leave them out. Writing a book has its moments of agony, let's be honest. I had vital encouragement and feedback at key times from Tom Adeyoola, Jamie Bartlett, Louise Chester, Andrew Davidson, Emma Gilpin-Jacobs, Henry Chevallier Guild, Charles Handy, Arianna Huffington, Herminia Ibarra, John Kelly, Gemma Lines, Sophie Levey, Joy Lo Dico, Emma Nelson, Bridget Nicholls, Tony Manwaring, Jessica Morris, Tanya Murphy, Hermian Murinik, Laline Paull, Matt Peacock, Rimma Perlmutter, Evelyn Reynold, Harry Ritchie, Stefan Stern, Jack Stoerger and Rachael Ward. Thank you for coating any iron comments in velvet gloves… and to Liz de

Planta whose painting *Horse Chestnut in Summer* in her tree series 'Look Up' I treated myself to buying when the book was finally finished: thank you, my friend.

Finally, to Brian and Elliott at Momento Print in London's Crouch End: I charted my book's progress by the thickness of each version they kindly printed out. To the Psycle team at Mortimer Street, London, especially AD Lemon and Cescie for all their brilliant energy; to Jen Palmer-Violet and Rupal Kantaria for their steady stream of hexagon photos and objects: so heartening! And finally, as always, all the team in The Juice Bar at The Lab in Muswell Hill who kept the coffee coming at my corner table as I wrote, head down, headphones on, but always looked up to a smile.

NOTES

Introduction

1 M Kaku. *The Future of the Mind: The scientific quest to understand, enhance, and empower the mind*, Doubleday, 2014
2 L Schenkman. In the brain, seven is a magic number, Inside Science, 23 November 2009
3 See more about Social Health on thriveglobal.com.
4 'Tri'. How you can train your brain to create new habits, Examined Existence blog, no date

1 Keeping your balance

1 J Schultz. How much data is created on the internet each day? Micro Focus blog, 6 August 2019
2 D A Norman. *Living with Complexity*, MIT Press, 2016
3 T Harford. *Messy: How to be creative and resilient in a tidy-minded world*, Little, Brown, 2018
4 M Maeterlinck. *The Life of the Bee*, Blue Ribbon Books (New York), 1901
5 *Health and safety at work: Summary statistics for Great Britain 2018*, Health and Safety Executive
6 T Cox, A J Griffiths and E Rial-Gonzalez. *Research on Work-related Stress*. Report to the European Agency for Safety and Health at Work, 2000
7 Calculating the cost of work-related stress and psychosocial risks, European Risk Observatory Literature Review, 2014
8 Suicide: One person dies every 40 seconds, World Health Organization, 2019

9 N Karlis. Why we feel anxious without knowing why, *Salon*, 24 January 2019

10 M Bunge. The complexity of simplicity, *Journal of Philosophy*, 59 (5), 1962

11 L Jackson and R Cracknell. Road accident casualties in Britain and the world, UK Parliament Research briefings, 2018

12 World Health Organization. Mobile phone use: A growing problem of driver distraction, 2011

2 Six packs

1 M McKay. The hexagon (a eulogy), Misfits' Architecture blog, 2 April 2018

2 The number 6 is called 'perfect' because it is equal to the sum of its factors. In other words, $1 + 2 + 3 = 1 \times 2 \times 3$.

3 Richard Fitzpatrick's parallel translation of Euclid's *Elements of Geometry* is available to download free from the University of Texas at Austin

4 First written about in 1955 by G A Miller: The magical number seven, plus or minus two: Some limits on our capacity for processing information, *Psychological Review*, 63 (2), 1956

5 A A Milne. *Now We Are Six*, Methuen, 1927

6 M Rees. *Just Six Numbers: The deep forces that shape the universe*, Orion Books, 2004

7 L Margonelli. *Underbug: An obsessive tale of termites and technology*, Scientific American/Farrar Straus & Giroux, 2018

8 C J H Concio. Bees declared to be the most important living being on earth, *Science Times*, 9 July 2019

9 L Paull. *The Bees*, Fourth Estate, 2015

10 Saturn's Hexagon could be an enormous tower, astronomy.com, 2018; L N Fletcher, G S Orton, J A Sinclair *et al*, A hexagon in Saturn's northern stratosphere surrounding the emerging summertime polar vortex, *Nature Communications*, 3 September 2018

11 K Vyas. Why is the hexagon everywhere? All about this seemingly common shape, *Interesting Engineering*, 10 June 2018

12 Bee behaviour, farmprogress.com

13 T D Seeley. *Honey Bee Democracy*, Princeton University Press, 2010

14 T Edwardes. *The Lore of the Honey-bee*, Methuen, 1919

3 From principle to practice

1 *Digital Information World*, 4 February 2019

2 P Ball. Why nature prefers boundaries, *Nautilus*, 7 April 2016

4 Side 1: Clarity

1 S Godin. You don't need more time, Seth's Blog, 9 February 2011

2 B Schwartz. *The Paradox of Choice: Why more is less*, Harper Perennial, 2015

3 S S Lyengar and M Lepper. When choice is demotivating: Can one desire too much of a good thing? *Journal of Personality and Social Psychology*, 79 (6), 2000

4 D Eagleman. *The Brain: The story of you*, Vintage Books (New York), 2017

5 M Lewis. Obama's Way. *Vanity Fair*, 11 September 2012

6 G Parker and L Hughes. European elections: Brexit party storms to victory in UK, *Financial Times*, 27 May 2019

7 *Communications Market Report*, Ofcom, 2018

8 M Curtin. Are you on your phone too much? The average person spends this many hours on it every day, *Inc*, 30 October 2018

9 E Ophir, C Nass and A D Wagner. Cognitive control in media multitaskers, Proceedings of the National Academy of Sciences, September 2009

10 G Mark, D Judith and U Klocke. The cost of interrupted work: More speed and stress, Proceedings of the 2008 Conference on Human Factors in Computing Systems, Florence

11   M Boland. Allostatic overload: Stress and emotional context
     Part I, Rebel Performance blog, 21 July 2017

12   B A Primack, A Shensa, J E Sidani, E O Whaite, L Y Liu, D Rosen,
     J B Colditz, A Radovic and E Miller. Social media use and
     perceived social isolation among young adults in the US,
     American Journal of Preventive Medicine, 53 (1), July 2017

13   Royal Society for Public Health. #StatusOfMind: Social media
     and young people's mental health and wellbeing, 2017

14   One example of reports on the value of habit to mental health:
     M Plata, The power of routines in your mental health,
     Psychology Today, 4 October 2018

15   S R Covey. *The Seven Habits of Highly Effective People*,
     Simon & Schuster, 1989

16   J Clear. *Atomic Habits: An easy and proven way to build good
     habits and break bad ones*, Penguin, 2018

17   H Villarica. The chocolate-and-radish experiment that birthed the
     modern conception of willpower, *The Atlantic*, 9 April 2012

18   N Eyal. Have we been thinking about willpower the wrong way
     for 30 years? *Harvard Business Review*, 23 November 2016

19   R H Thaler. *Misbehaving: The making of behavioral economics*,
     Norton, 2016

20   T Ferris. *The 4-Hour Body: An uncommon guide to rapid fat-loss,
     incredible sex and becoming superhuman*, Ebury Publishing, 2011

21   Glassdoor again ranks Kronos an employees' choice best place to
     work, Kronos Incorporated, 2018

22   J Maeda. *The Laws of Simplicity*, MIT Press, 2006

23   *Behavioural Insights and Public Policy: Lessons from around the
     world*, OECD, 2017

24   S Lakhotia. Gig economy: A boon for women, *Entrepreneur*,
     24 May 2019

25   D Allen. *Getting Things Done: The art of stress-free productivity*,
     Penguin, 2001

26   *2019 European Self Storage Survey*, Federation of European
     Self Storage Associations

27 Global self storage market size, share, trends, CAGR by technology, key players, regions, cost, revenue and forecast to 2024, Analytical Research Cognizance, 23 July 2019

28 J Wallman. *Stuffocation: Living more with less: How we've had enough of stuff and why you need experience more than ever*, Crux Publishing, 2015

29 S Begley. The Science of Making Decisions, *Newsweek*, 27 February 2011

30 S Bates. A decade of data reveals that heavy multitaskers have reduced memory, Stanford psychologist says, *Stanford News*, 25 October 2018

5 Side 2: Individuality

1 How do snowflakes form? Get the science behind snow, National Oceanic and Atmospheric Administration, 2016

2 B R Little. Personal projects and free traits: Personality and motivation reconsidered, *Social and Personality Psychology Compass*, 2/3, April 2008

3 B R Little. *Me, Myself and Us: The science of personality and the art of well-being*, Public Affairs (New York), 2016

4 J Hobsbawm. Overcoming digital distraction, *Strategy+Business*, 23 January 2019

5 S Salim. More than six hours of our day is spent online, *Digital Information World*, 4 February 2019

6 R Bharadwaj. AI for identity theft protection in banking, *Emerj*, 16 August 2019

7 R Siciliano. Youth suicide on the rise… Is social media to blame? Safr.me blog, 9 May 2019

8 C Warzel. Could restorative justice fix the internet? *New York Times*, 20 August 2019

9 OCEAN personality types (the Big Five traits), Vision One, 26 June 2016

10 T Grandin and R Panek. *The Autistic Brain: Thinking across the spectrum*, Houghton Mifflin Harcourt, 2013

11   teamdomenica.com

12   L Devine. Princess Diana's goddaughter, 24, reveals she spoiled her family after receiving her first ever pay cheque, *The Sun*, 2 September 2019

13   johnscrazysocks.com

14   Moai Capital

15   T Tharp. *The Creative Habit: Learn it and use it for life*, Simon & Schuster, 2018

16   D Bledsoe. Screenwriting with impact: 6 tips for vastly improving your scripts, *Freelance Writing* (no date)

17   P Belton. My robot makes me feel like I haven't been forgotten, BBC News Business, 31 August 2018

18   W Smale. How rude service inspired a multi-million euro firm, BBC News Business, 1 July 2019

19   M J Poulin and E A Holman, Helping hands, healthy body? Oxytocin receptor gene and prosocial behavior interact to buffer the association between stress and physical health, *Hormones and Behavior*, 63 (1), March 2013

6   Side 3: Reset

1   J Odell. *How to Do Nothing: Resisting the attention economy*, Melville House Publishing, 2019

2   O Moshfegh. *My Year of Rest and Relaxation*, Jonathan Cape, 2018

3   E Pofeldt. Are we ready for a workforce that is 50% freelance? *Forbes*, 17 October 2017

4   *Accelerating Workforce Reskilling for the Fourth Industrial Revolution*, World Economic Forum, 2017

5   J Hari. *Chasing the Scream: The first and last days of the war on drugs*, Bloomsbury, 2015

6   A Huffington. *Thrive: The third metric to redefining success and creating a life of well-being, wisdom, and wonder*, Harmony, 2014

7 F Jabr. Why your brain needs more downtime, *Scientific American*, 15 October 2013

8 A Pillay. Secret to brain success: Intelligent cognitive rest, Harvard Health Blog, 4 May 2017

9 M Pollan. *How to Change Your Mind: What the new science of psychedelics teaches us about consciousness, dying, addiction, depression, and transcendence*, Penguin, 2018

10 H Jury. How travel can benefit our mental health, Psych Central blog, 8 July 2018

11 H J Wadey. *The Bee Craftsman: A short guide to the life story and management of the honey-bee*, A G Smith, 1945

12 J Suttie. How nature can make you kinder, happier, and more creative, Greater Good Science Center at UC Berkeley, 2 March 2016

13 S D'Souza, and D Renner. *Not Doing: The art of effortless action*, LID Publishing, 2018

14 M van den Berg, J Maas, R Muller, A Braun, W Kaandorp, R van Lien and A van den Berg. Autonomic nervous system responses to viewing green and built settings: Differentiating between sympathetic and parasympathetic activity, *International Journal of Environmental Research and Public Health*, 12 (12), 2015

15 A W Brooks. Emotion and the art of negotiation, *Harvard Business Review*, 93 (12), December 2015

16 S D Pressman, K A Matthews, S Cohen, L M Martire, M Scheier, A Baum and R Schulz. Association of enjoyable leisure activities with psychological and physical well-being, *Psychosomatic Medicine*, 71 (7), September 2009

17 D Sgroi. Happiness and productivity: Understanding the happy-productive worker, Social Market Foundation and Foundation for Competitive Advantage in the Global Economy, 2015

18 How's life? 2017: Measuring well-being, OECD, 2017

7 Side 4: Knowledge

1   M Haig @matthaig1. Twitter, 27 May 2019
2   T Klingberg. *The Overflowing Brain*, Oxford University Press, 2009
3   J Szalay. Camel spiders: Facts and myths, *Live Science*, 17 December 2014
4   M Gladwell. *Talking to Strangers: What we should know about the people we don't know*, Allen Lane, 2019
5   J Bartlett. *The Missing Cryptoqueen*, podcast, 2019
6   D A Norman. *Living with Complexity,* MIT Press, 2016
7   R B Cialdini. *Influence: The psychology of persuasion*, HarperCollins, 1993
8   P Ashcroft and G Jones. *Alive: Digital humans and their organizations*, Novaro Publishing, 2018
9   K Szczepanski. The invention of the saddle stirrup, ThoughtCo, 3 July 2019
10 W Lipmann. *Liberty and the News*, Harcourt, Brace and Howe, 1920
11 *The New Digital Workplace Divide*, Unisys, 2018
12 D Rumsfeld. US Department of Defense news briefing, 12 February 2002
13 R Harris. Death by PowerPoint, Zdnet, 29 April 2010
14 J F Messier. What if NASA had not used PowerPoint in 2003? New Sales Presentation blog, 27 April 2019
15 'Jamie'. Death by PowerPoint: the slide that killed seven people, McDreeamie Musings blog, 15 April 2019
16 N N Taleb. *The Black Swan: The impact of the highly improbable*, Penguin, 2010
17 A Smith. Interview with Andre Geim, Nobel Foundation, 5 October 2010
18 N N Taleb. *Fooled by Randomness: The hidden role of chance in life and in the markets*, Penguin, 2007
19 P Illanes, S Lund, M Mourshed, S Rutherford and M Tyreman. Retraining and reskilling workers in the age of automation, McKinsey Global Institute, 2018
20 National Qualities Index, Qdooz, 2019

21 L S A Kwapong, E Opoku and F Donyina. The effect of motivation on the performance of teaching staff in Ghanaian polytechnics: The moderating role of education and research experience, *International Journal of Education and Research*, 3 (11), November 2015

22 *Obesity and overweight*, World Health Organization, February 2018

23 R J Yun, J H Krystal and D H Mathalon. Working memory overload: Fronto-limbic interactions and effects on subsequent working memory function, *Brain Imaging Behaviour*, 4 (1), March 2010

8 Side 5: Networks

1 K Nanjiani. Commencement Address at Grinnell College, Iowa, 22 May 2017

2 M D Lieberman. *Social: Why our brains are wired to connect*, Oxford University Press, 2013

3 S Kemp. Digital 2019: Global internet use accelerates, We Are Social blog, 30 January 2019

4 P Wohlleben. *The Hidden Life of Trees: What they feel, how they communicate*, William Collins, 2015

5 J Hobsbawm. *Fully Connected: Social health in an age of overload*, Bloomsbury Business, 2018

6 R I M Dunbar. Do online social media cut through the constraints that limit the size of offline social networks? Royal Society Open Science, 1 January 2016

7 E Cirino. What are the benefits of hugging? *Healthline*, 10 April 2018

8 T Hanson. *Buzz: The nature and neccesity of bees*, Icon, 2018

9 S Kesebir. The superorganism account of human sociality: How and when human groups are like beehives, *Personality and Social Psychology Review*, 16 (3), 2011

10 A L Barabasi and E Bonabeau. Scale-free networks, *Scientific American*, May 2003

11 M R Roghanizad and V K Bohns. Ask in person: You're less persuasive than you think over email, *Journal of Experimental Social Psychology*, 69, March 2016

12 F Laloux. *Reinventing Organizations: A guide to creating organizations inspired by the next stage of human consciousness*, Nelson Parker (Brussels)

13 T Standage. *Writing on the Wall: Social media – the first 2,000 years*, Bloomsbury, 2014

14 marnitastable.org

9 Side 6: Time

1 S Kemp. Digital in 2018: World's internet users pass the 4 billion mark, We Are Social blog, 30 January 2018

2 Internet Stats & Facts for 2019, Hosting Facts blog, 17 December 2018

3 Y N Harari. *21 Lessons for the 21st Century*, Jonathan Cape, 2018

4 B Nelson. The world's 10 oldest living trees, Mother Nature Network, 27 October 2016

5 S Godin. Lesson's for telling time, Seth's Blog, 26 February 2019. I recommend reading anything and everything by Seth Godin.

6 E J Langer and J Rodine. The effects of choice and enhanced personal responsibility for the aged: A field experiment in an institutional setting. *Journal of Personality and Social Psychology*, 34 (2), August 1976

7 B Chapman. What happened when Sweden tried six-hour working days, *The Independent*, 10 February 2107

8 S Boseley. Too much overtime is bad for your health, says study, *The Guardian*, 11 May 2010

9 *The Future of Jobs: Employment, skills and workforce strategy for the Fourth Industrial Revolution* World Economic Forum, 2016

10 E Pofeldt. Are we ready for a workforce that is 50% freelance? *Forbes*, 17 October 2017

11 R Jay. 5 etiquette rules for working across time zones, Remote.co, 5 March 2018

12 A Ain. *Work Inspired: How to build an organization where everybody loves to work*, McGraw-Hill, 2019

13 C Newport. *Deep Work: Rules for focused success in a distracted world*, Piatkus, 2016

14 F Laloux. *Reinventing Organizations: A guide to creating organizations inspired by the next stage of human consciousness*, Nelson Parker (Brussels), 2014

15 B Daisley (2019) *The Joy of Work: 30 ways to fix your work culture and fall in love with your job again*, Random House, 2019

16 S-J Blakemore. *Inventing Ourselves: The secret life of the teenage brain*, Black Swan, 2019

17 C Rovelli. Time travel is just what we do every day, *The Guardian*, 31 March 2019

18 J Wajcman *Pressed for Time: The acceleration of life in digital capitalism*, University of Chicago Press, 2015

19 S Burkhart in: J O'Donnell Maroney. *Being Present: A practical guide for transforming the employee experience of your frontline workforce*, The Workforce Institute at Kronos, 2019

10 Six Hexagon Thinkers

1 F Osier. The Key to a better vaccine. TED talk, April 2018

2 N Pullman. A simple life, Wicked Leeks blog, 22 August 2019

3 A Norris. 11 intriguing basalt columns around the world, From the Grapevine, 1 October 2014

4 A Huffington. *The Sleep Revolution: Transforming your life, one night at a time*, Penguin Random House, 2016

5 ourbrainbank.org

6 G Thunberg. *No One Is Too Small to Make a Difference*, Penguin, 2019

7 J Henley. #stayontheground: Swedes turn to trains amid climate 'flight shame', *The Guardian*, 4 June 2019

11   Be the bee

1   J Françon. *The Mind of the Bees*, Methuen, 1947
2   L Margonelli. *Underbug: An obsessive tale of termites and technology,* Scientific American/Farrar Straus & Giroux, 2018

12   Six-Fixes + 6

1   F Macdonald. Scientists have made a diamond that's harder than diamond, Science Alert, 13 December 2016
2   S Salim. More than six hours of our day is spent online, *Digital Information World*, 4 February 2019

FURTHER READING

A Ain. *Work Inspired: How to build an organization where everybody loves to work*, McGraw-Hill, 2019

D Allen. *Getting Things Done: The art of stress-free productivity*, Penguin, 2001

P Ashcroft and G Jones. *Alive: Digital humans and their organizations*, Novaro Publishing, 2018

S-J Blakemore. *Inventing Ourselves: The secret life of the teenage brain*, Black Swan, 2019

S Burkhart in: J O'Donnell Maroney. *Being Present: A practical guide for transforming the employee experience of your frontline workforce*, The Workforce Institute at Kronos, 2019

R B Cialdini. *Influence: The psychology of persuasion*, HarperCollins, 1993

J Clear. *Atomic Habits: An easy and proven way to build good habits and break bad ones*, Penguin, 2018

S R Covey. *The Seven Habits of Highly Effective People*, Simon & Schuster, 1989

B Daisley (2019) *The Joy of Work: 30 ways to fix your work culture and fall in love with your job again*, Random House, 2019

S D'Souza, and D Renner. *Not Doing: The art of effortless action*, LID Publishing, 2018

D Eagleman. *The Brain: The story of you*, Vintage Books (New York), 2017

T Edwardes. *The Lore of the Honeybee*, Methuen, 1937

Euclid's *Elements of Geometry* in a parallel translation by Richard Fitzpatrick is available to download free from the University of Texas at Austin

T Ferris. *The 4-Hour Body: An uncommon guide to rapid fat-loss, incredible sex and becoming superhuman*, Ebury Publishing, 2011

J Françon. *The Mind of the Bees*, Methuen, 1947

M Gladwell. *Talking to Strangers: What we should know about the people we don't know*, Allen Lane, 2019

T Grandin and R Panek. *The Autistic Brain: Thinking across the spectrum*, Houghton Mifflin Harcourt, 2013

T Hanson. *Buzz: The nature and neccesity of bees*, Icon, 2018

Y N Harari. *21 Lessons for the 21st Century*, Jonathan Cape, 2018

T Harford. *Messy: How to be creative and resilient in a tidy-minded world*, Little, Brown, 2018

J Hari. *Chasing the Scream: The first and last days of the war on drugs*, Bloomsbury, 2015

J Hobsbawm. *Fully Connected: Social health in an age of overload*, Bloomsbury Business, 2018

A Huffington. *The Sleep Revolution: Transforming your life, one night at a time*, Penguin Random House, 2016

A Huffington. *Thrive: The third metric to redefining success and creating a life of well-being, wisdom, and wonder*, Harmony, 2014

M Kaku. *The Future of the Mind: The scientific quest to understand, enhance, and empower the mind*, Doubleday, 2014

T Klingberg. *The Overflowing Brain*, Oxford University Press, 2009

M D Lieberman. *Social: Why our brains are wired to connect*, Oxford University Press, 2013

W Lipmann. *Liberty and the News*, Harcourt, Brace and Howe, 1920

B R Little. *Me, Myself and Us: The science of personality and the art of well-being*, Public Affairs (New York), 2016

J Maeda. *The Laws of Simplicity*, MIT Press, 2006

M Maeterlinck. *The Life of the Bee*, Blue Ribbon Books (New York)

L Margonelli. *Underbug: An obsessive tale of termites and technology*, Scientific American/Farrar Straus & Giroux, 2018

A A Milne. *Now We Are Six*, Methuen, 1927

O Moshfegh. *My Year of Rest and Relaxation*, Jonathan Cape, 2018

The New Digital Workplace Divide, Unisys, 2018

C Newport. *Deep Work: Rules for focused success in a distracted world*, Piatkus, 2016

D A Norman. *Living with Complexity*, MIT Press, 2016

J Odell. *How to Do Nothing: Resisting the attention economy*, Melville House Publishing, 2019

L Paull. *The Bees, Fourth Estate*, 2015

M Pollan. *How to Change Your Mind: What the new science of psychedelics teaches us about consciousness, dying, addiction, depression, and transcendence*, Penguin, 2018

M Rees. *Just Six Numbers: The deep forces that shape the universe*, Orion Books, 2004

B Schwartz. *The Paradox of Choice: Why more is less*, Harper Perennial, 2015

T D Seeley. *Honey Bee Democracy*, Princeton University Press, 2010

T Standage. *Writing on the Wall: Social media – the first 2,000 years*, Bloomsbury, 2014

N N Taleb. *The Black Swan: The impact of the highly improbable*, Penguin, 2010

N N Taleb. *Fooled by Randomness: The hidden role of chance in life and in the markets*, Penguin, 2007

R H Thaler. *Misbehaving: The making of behavioral economics*, Norton, 2016

T Tharp. *The Creative Habit: Learn it and use it for life*, Simon & Schuster, 2006

G Thunberg. *No One is Too Small to Make a Difference*, Penguin, 2019

H J Wadey. *The Bee Craftsman: A short guide to the life story and management of the honey-bee*, A G Smith, 1945

J Wajcman. *Pressed for Time: The acceleration of life in digital capitalism*, University of Chicago Press, 2015

J Wallman. *Stuffocation: Living more with less: How we've had enough of stuff and why you need experience more than ever*, Crux Publishing, 2015

P Wohlleben. *The Hidden Life of Trees: What they feel, how they communicate*, William Collins, 2015

INDEX